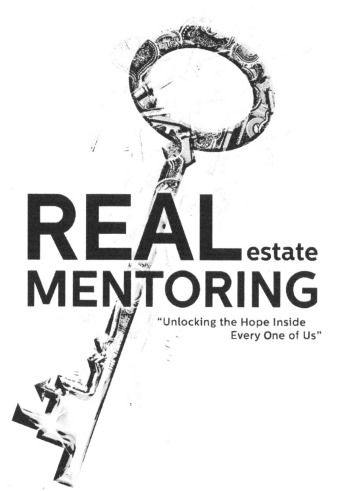

REAL estate
MENTORING

"Unlocking the Hope Inside
Every One of Us"

Real Estate Mentoring

By Steve Burris

Copyright © 2021 Steve Burris

Edited by: Andrea Pflughoft & Calley Overton

Cover Design: Scott Soliz, www.zealdesino.com

ISBN-13: 978-1736707067

CEDAR GATE
PUBLISHING

Dedication

This book is dedicated to my wife Brandi who always stood behind me and pushed me in her own strength, and to all of our Kevo leadership who believed in our mission and paved the way for everyone else!

Table of Contents

Introduction

Welcome home! It's a phrase REALTORS® look forward to saying every time they link an individual or family with the home of their dreams. Home. Songs and books of all kinds remind us there's no place like it.

In the times we're living, home is not always traditional—where you have a mortgage and you "own" your home. Nowadays, leasing/renting is common and can be the perfect fit for someone, and whatever the reason, they prefer that option. Depending on where you live, a suburban house, condo dwelling, or downtown apartment might be your style.

More than likely, when you began a search for your version of "home," it was a REALTOR® who helped you.

Here's an amazing thought: in spite of all that has changed throughout the years when it comes to real estate, very little has changed in the manner in which real estate agents are licensed and trained. In fact, if you are an agent reading this right now, you're probably shaking your head in agreement and yelling, "Steve! Nothing has changed!" You'd be right, my friend.

This is why Kevo Properties exists! We exist to turn the real estate industry on its head. We left the traditional way of thinking behind and we bring those dejected and disposable agents to the front.

How do we do this? We put REALTORS® first! We give REALTORS® the highest level of training, mentorship, and team support. Success follows!

I believe you are reading this book because:

A) You are new to the industry and you're broken financially, mentally, emotionally, and spiritually.

B) You have been in the industry for some amount of time, but still can't figure out why you seem to be one step behind all the time.

C) You are interested in the business because someone has told you about all the money you'll make even just working a few hours a month.

D) You aren't a REALTOR®, but you're struggling to make it through your life because some bad times or bad people have made you doubt your calling.

E) Someone handed it to you and said, "Read this!"

I'm telling my story because I know what all the above feel like. I've lived in every one of them. When it comes to our tough times in life, there are some things we just cannot control. Tough times happen. Sometimes they come from our own making and sometimes not. Tough times may come, but they won't stay forever. I'm proof! That's good news, right? There's an old saying, "Tough times don't last; tough people do."

Here is more good news: your failure in real estate is not your fault! Let me repeat that. It's not your fault! The reason you are not making it in the real estate industry is simple. Agents fail because the entire system has set them up for failure. So, what has happened before you picked up my book is not your fault. But—and this is a big "but"—if you don't make some changes after reading my book, your failure will be your fault.

I invite you to open the door of your mind and heart and allow me to be your guide.

Welcome home to the incredible world of real estate!

CHAPTER 1

There's No Place Like Home

"Buyers decide in the first eight seconds of seeing a home if they're interested in buying it. Get out of your car, walk in their shoes, and see what they see within the first eight seconds."

-Barbara Corcoran

"Home, Sweet Home"
John Howard Payne (1823)

'Mid pleasures and palaces though we may roam,
Be it ever so humble, there's no place like home.
A charm from the skies seems to hallow us there,
Which, seek through the world, is ne'er met elsewhere.

Home! Home!
Sweet, sweet home!
There's no place like home,
There's no place like home!

Words spoken through the lyrics of John Howard Payne and repeated by Dorothy in The Wizard of Oz echo the sentiment so many of us feel: "There's no place like home." You've seen it stitched on a wall hanging or pillow, or quoted in various ways throughout time, and yet no matter how magnificent a vacation or no matter the state of our home, we all breathe a sigh of relief when we arrive through the doors of "Home."

You need a license to drive, cut hair, sell insurance, and sell a home. What makes the difference between success and failure in any of those areas? Training. You can read, take a test, and call yourself an agent, but you won't stay one for long without proper training. Trust me. I know.

How many times have we heard of the star that seems to hit it big with one song? Some of you may be familiar with an Oklahoma icon named Garth Brooks. Before his first "hit song," few people realized the hours he traveled back and forth from Oklahoma to Nashville trying to make it in the music industry. Only a handful of people were with him to see the lean bank account and the struggles. Everyone saw the success, even if you weren't a country music fan.

According to Malcolm Gladwell in his book Outliers: The Story of Success, it takes ten thousand hours of practice to master something. Since there are over 8,700 hours in one year, even if you spent twenty-four hours a day trying to master something, you would still need about 1.5 years. I have never measured the number of hours I have personally spent learning and mastering what it takes to make it in real estate, but it far exceeds ten thousand hours. Many look at my success now and think, "Well, I'll get my real estate license and make it big like Steve-O!" To be totally honest, it's not likely. Unless you are linked with a company like mine, you would be better off to save your money and time and choose a different career. Why? Because out of the one hundred people who will get their license, eighty-seven will fail. That's the harsh reality of real estate. However, if you have the dream to be successful in real estate and you want to learn, I'm your guy!

I started trying to make money in the real estate industry twenty-five years ago. Like most Americans, I was living paycheck to paycheck. I had a full-time job at a drugstore (by the way, that isn't code for a CBD store–it was an actual pharmacy). When I found my first house to flip, I bought it for $45,000. I moved my family in, made some improvements, and then sold it for a profit. After six months of investing my money, time, and labor, I was able to sell the house for $78,000. After deducting the costs of improvements, my profit was about $7,000. That amount of money was a big deal for me! The REALTOR® who listed the house earned $2,400. I had just spent six months sweating through evenings and weekends to rehab this house, and she rolled up in a Cadillac, stuck a sign in the yard, and, thirty-four days later, walked away with a couple thousand dollars. Her version of earning money seemed much easier than mine.

Two months later, I had my real estate license. I knew I was going to make it big! I joined a large brokerage firm and quit my job at the pharmacy company. Two years after that, I owed the brokerage firm $6,400. Yes, you read that right. I OWED THEM MONEY! I had sold so few homes that I was actually in debt with the brokerage.

When a new agent starts in the real estate business, they pay the brokerage a portion of their sales commission. They also have to pay monthly fees for desk space, transaction assistance, and other general office needs. I sold so few properties in those first two years that I was unable even to cover the base expenses of working the business. I saw the beginning of what I now consider a broken real estate system.

It became clear that the real estate system was not designed for someone like me. Who is "someone like me?" Well, I'm the guy that barely made it out of high school. I took algebra four times and was glad to finally get a passing grade (thankfully a 'D' counts as passing). No college for Steve-O. Actually, my uncle helped get me that job with the pharmacy company. I was doing exactly what I had watched my dad do: Get up, go to work, come home, get up, go to work, come home, and repeat until one day you retire with enough money to pay the bills. There's nothing wrong with working hard and working a "regular" job. The USA was built on hard-working, good men and women who worked like my dad. That's who I was … a hard-working, good guy. It's just that I had no real plan for the future. Did I quit real estate? Hell no! I was too stubborn for that. But I did have to swallow my pride and ask for my full-time job back at the pharmacy. I stuck with the real estate business on a part-time basis.

Over the next three years, still only working the business part-time, I actually figured out how to make great money in real estate. I also figured out all the pitfalls new agents step into. As I cover those pitfalls in the next chapters, I think it will be clear to you why 87 percent of all new agents fail within their first two years in the industry … Gone. Bye-bye. Out of business. That failure rate is way too big. I promise to show you why it's not your fault.

CHAPTER 2

Hard Knocks

"Real estate cannot be lost or stolen. Nor can it be carried away. Purchased with common sense, paid for in full, and managed with reasonable care, it is about the safest investment in the world."

-Franklin D. Roosevelt

There's an old saying, "Progress always involves risk; you can't steal second base and keep your foot on first." I was ready to make it big, or so I thought. I decided it was time to take the risk. Starting out, I thought I was completely qualified to do this since I was professionally trained on how to sell as a pharmaceutical sales rep. However, none of that ended up mattering.

I went to work for RE/MAX. I was friends with both of the owners, a husband-and-wife team. The wife, Anita, was making over $300,000 a year, and I thought that would be the perfect place to work. It was five minutes from my house. I could go there every day, see the people in the office, and do open houses. Time was ticking away on me making any money. It took me six or seven months to just get my first listing.

That first listing was a nightmare. The owner had no money and the house was a wreck. He had two giant dogs and it was obvious that he never let them outside. You can just imagine what the carpets were like, and whatever you can imagine, it was much worse. It was bad—as in "gagging" bad! To add insult to injury, at the time, outdoor signs were $55. It made me sick that I was going to have to spend more money to get a listing. I finally had something I could actually make money on, but I had to spend even more money just for the opportunity. I can see some of you nodding your head "yes" as you're reading this right now!

The bottom line was it was time to get to work to sell it. "Work" was the keyword here. We rolled up all the carpets and rugs and put them in the garage. That way you could at least breathe in the house to be able to show it. I should have purchased stock in some sort of deodorizer or "odor eater." We decided the best route was to try to sell it using a Federal Housing Administration (FHA) loan. However, FHA requires houses to have carpeting. When the FHA appraiser came to the house, we just rolled the carpet back into all the rooms. Can you imagine? The smell was overwhelming, but somehow it ended up qualifying and the house sold. I made $1,300-$1,400 on the sale, but I still owed RE/MAX over $4,000.

The part about the condition of the house may have made you

chuckle, and, looking back, I can laugh too. However, at the time, I was sinking financially. And I was not an anomaly. You either know someone or you are the someone who has likely had this type of result as a real estate agent.

Another twelve months went by. I was even more financially in the hole, and I was working open houses every Sunday. I had a lady client who had just gotten a divorce. She needed to sell her $300,000 house, but I could tell she didn't have enough equity in the house to get the standard 6 percent commission rate. Going into the business, I knew there were going to be many people in that same situation. I went to my broker and explained the situation and told him I wanted to drop the rate down to 4.5 percent in order for the sale to go through. I figured making some money was better than nothing, plus I would be helping somebody out. What do you think happened?

If you guessed my broker agreed with me, you guessed wrong. Even all these years later, I still remember getting chewed out for supposedly lowering my standards as a professional. He said if I lowered my rate, I would wreck the entire industry. No joke! In fact, the client's own sister was an agent and couldn't help her since she wasn't allowed to go below 6 percent. Sad. On top of all that, I literally heard comments from multiple people saying, "If you start dropping your rate, you'll ruin everything! You'll wreck all of us!" And I kept thinking I couldn't believe this one house was going to wreck us all!

At this point, I still wasn't making money. I explained to my broker I was going to have to quit and get a full-time job. He told me not to worry about it, that I'd catch up. I waited two months, and I only had another $1,200-$1,300 to go towards my debt. I finally had to face reality and get a different job. For the next three years, I had to figure out how to do real estate while working a full-time job. It was really a blessing though because it was another fifteen years before Kevo Properties would open.

During this time, I got into the business of flipping houses. I was working full time for Hobby Lobby, and the real estate gig was part time. I knew how to put a house together to make it look its best. I also had a good work ethic.

I had gotten to the level of flipping houses that I ended up meeting a multi-millionaire named Dan. On my own, I could only flip one or two houses at a time. After I met Dan, he started backing my purchases, and at one point, I had $5 million in flip houses. Even with that success, I knew my heart was somewhere else—selling houses, not flipping them. I decided it was time to quit my job to do real estate full time.

Before I opened Kevo Properties, I tried opening my own agency under a different name. I worked full time for Hobby Lobby, so I hired a commercial broker to run the business and then taught him how to do residential real estate. I recruited twenty-five to thirty REALTORS® to work for me. For the next two years, this broker ran the business.

On his own, he changed the company name and website to something he controlled. He fundamentally controlled everything at that point since he was the broker and told me we were going to renegotiate. He demanded that I cut my REALTORS®' salaries in half and give that money to him instead. Basically, he embezzled the company. That's when I realized I had to be involved full time, including being the broker, or it wasn't going to work.

This was a "fork in the road" moment. Would I quit my job and be "all-in," which would mean getting my broker's license and owning my company, or would I stay in the business world, working for a great company like Hobby Lobby? I was married, so this was not just about me.

At one point, I had been single for ten years, but then I met Brandi. Two years after meeting her, we were married. From the time I met her, she has always been 100 percent behind me, a true cheerleader. She was a nail technician and part-owner of a salon. I explained to her I wanted to devote myself full time to real estate. She immediately told me to go for it. She said she knew I'd be great at whatever I did. It's true what the Bible says in Proverbs 31, a good woman is hard to find and her worth is far more than jewels.

I found a diamond when I met Brandi.

With her full support, I quit my job with Hobby Lobby and started the process of getting my broker's license. We pulled out all the money we had in my 401(k), around $70,000. After the penalties, we ended up with around $50,000. With these funds, we opened the doors of Kevo Properties in January of 2011. I had three agents, a one-person office staff, and myself. The opening starting cost to run the office was almost $7,000 a month.

The name Kevo came with help from Darren Wilson. I met Darren through a friend of mine, Kent Long. Darren did advertising for A+ Online Schools and had a staff of around one hundred people. He decided to do freelance work on the side to help out his brother, who was a chiropractor. Kent introduced us and he agreed to take me on as a client also. We worked together for about four months and came up with the name Kevo. I'm am often asked, "What does 'Kevo' mean?" Was it my middle name or nickname? Kevo was born out of the collaboration of myself and one guy and his team. Darren was a guy I met through another friend of mine. Darren was this big shot with a large global company. He was their marketing VP. He heard that I was starting a new company and asked if I wanted help. He was sick of traveling for his job. His son had told another friend that his dad worked at the airport. When Darren asked his son why he said that, his son said, "Well, that's where we always drop you off and pick you up." Darren knew then he had to get out. He said that most small business owners never have the resorces like a big company to launch a business with the right marketing strategy. Darren was thinking he could start a small company and help other small companies get started. He had just finished helping his brother launch a national online platform for his chiropractic program. I would be his second client and last.

Darren and I started with what would be the name. This was a two-month process to come up with the name. First, the name had to be simple and easy to remember. The name also had to mean nothing in the public's head when we said the name. Here's the reason: people think in terms of images not words. That's why companies like McDonald's, Nicki, and Apple put so much money into their logos. When you hear those companies, you always see the logo. I ask this question all the time about the McDonald's signs, which you have seen a thousand times. Under the big yellow arches, how is the company's name spelled? Is it "McDonalds" or "McDonald's"? You've seen it before, but if you're like most people you would not bet $500 on the one you thought for sure was right. Our job was to do the same thing.

Darren had a program that generated random words, some real and some just made up. We would look at the twenty or so names and pick out ones we liked. Then we would see if the name could be copyrighted and patent protected. Once the word "Kevo" was picked, then it would go into design and we would choose the fonts, the size, the color, and the logo. The font was chosen because it was very close to Darren's's fonts. The key and its design went all over the place. The older looking key tilted on its side would soften the name of "Kevo." The key also made it easy to pronounce Kevo.

In 2013, Quickset, a lock-making company, came up with a keyless home lock that was also called Kevo. It was funny, all my friends saw the new lock on the shelf and sent me photos asking if I had started making locks for Kevo. When I first started Kevo, I was not sure what the company would be known for. When you start a company, you can wish and hope for what your employees and the public will think about you. You just start out with the intention of helping people and trying to fix something you see as broken. I'm proud to say after ten years Kevo means transparency, commitment, and selflessness. Kevo is the place to help new agents be successful. After that, Darren decided he wasn't going to freelance anymore. He only had two clients, his brother and me.

Obviously naming a business is not all there is to owning a business. The first thirty days of the official Kevo Properties proved to be very difficult. I had to put another broker over Kevo for the first thirty days since I didn't have my broker's license yet. In those thirty days, my broker was named in a complaint from a real estate commissioner. I had to attend a meeting with the assistant attorney general and representatives from three other brokerage firms also named in the complaint. The whole thing nauseated me because we were already bleeding cash. I sat in the meeting thinking I only had my doors open for two months, and now I was going to be wrecked. I had no backup plan because once you leave Hobby Lobby, they won't rehire you. Thankfully, it was determined we didn't do anything wrong and we dodged that bullet.

CHAPTER 3

"I Know So Many People"

"Now, one thing I tell everyone is learn about real estate. Repeat after me: Real estate provides the highest returns, the greatest values, and the least risk."

-Armstrong Williams

New agents tell me all the time why they will be the one who will make it past the 87 percent failure rate. They tell me things like, "I love to stage houses!" "I love going to open houses!" and "I've got some great marketing ideas!" Every new idea will cost you money, I promise. Most of the ideas are good. It's just that none of them will help you make a penny in the real world of real estate unless you have worked your way into a deep network of contacts.

A full-time agent needs to make thirty to forty home sales a year to make a good living. The average home price in the United States is $240,000. If an agent also sells a few $500,000 houses here and there, they may not need to sell as many homes to make ends meet. Learn to accept this: if you are ever going to sell enough homes to make it in this industry, you absolutely must learn to network. That involves meeting lots of new people and getting them to like and trust you.

Networking sounds pretty simple, right? You just go to a luncheon and pass out business cards or tell all of your friends you're in real estate now. It may be simple, but it's not easy. The fact is, you have to go much deeper than you may realize. Think about this: How many close friends do you have? Stop and make a list of everyone you can think of, putting them into three different categories:

1. Family and close friends. These are people you can call or text and see them immediately.

2. Acquaintances. Not as close as your inner circle, but you can call and set up an appointment to see them.

3. Contacts. People you don't know very well, but that you may deal with somewhat regularly in a business capacity (doctors, dry cleaners, other business owners, etc.). You can email them your information.

When you tell all these people that you have a real estate license, they will all congratulate you on becoming a REALTOR®. But why would they use you? You're new, so they assume you know nothing about real estate. Think about going to a barber or hair salon and the person tells you they just finished cosmetology school and you're their first real customer. How confident would you be with their skills? Between the newbie and John or Julie, who've been cutting hair for twenty years, who would you naturally gravitate to chop your hair? So now, think about your friend or associate. Until now, they've only known you as a _____ (fill in the blank with whatever line of work you were in before real estate). They will barely consider you when looking for an agent.

You will have to do some deep networking to meet enough people who think of you as a bona fide real estate agent. You need to network into the lists you made above to get their list of contacts. Then network a little deeper into the next level of contacts and keep going. That's the only way you can get a big enough list to start actually making sales. Now you understand why I said it's simple, but not easy. Networking is not just a matter of telling people about your business.

Another aspect of networking is learning how to pick up clients from open houses. Sorry, that information won't be in this book. I'm saving it for my next book on the how-tos of real estate. Don't worry, you're going to learn plenty from this book to build your business. ... Let's move on!

Action: Make a list of everyone you know grouped into the three categories listed in this chapter ... family/close friends, acquaintances, contacts.

CHAPTER 4

You Can't Buy Your Way into Success

"Real estate is the best investment in the world, because it's the only thing they're not making anymore."

-Will Rogers

Agents who are buying leads are building a business that will not last long-term. I firmly believe if you're going to succeed in this business, you must take time to learn the skills that it takes to pick up your own buyer leads and listings. I feel so strongly about this because when you learn these skills, you will control your money, not someone else. Remember the old saying, "Give a man a fish and he'll eat for a day; teach him to fish and he'll eat for a lifetime." If an agent is taught to only buy leads, they will earn enough for a few days; but if an agent is taught to cultivate leads for themselves, they will earn enough for a lifetime.

Most agents I talk to don't take the time to do the math on whether buying leads or using new tactics will be profitable in the long run. It's called calculating your return on investment (ROI). I have spoken with agents who tell the stories. Many of them end up spending more money buying leads than they ever make from the commission on those leads. Determining your ROI just takes a simple math equation that most agents don't even try to figure out. The bottom line is that buying leads will not work out as profitable over many, many years.

There will always be some new tactic out there to gain clients. Still, those methods only work for a short time. I'm reminded of a drawing of two old miners trying to find the hidden gems in a mine. One is above the other, and they've been using their pick-axe to chop away the dirt, looking for the gems. It's grinding work, and after a while, the miner above the other one gives up and walks off. What we see, that neither miner can, is that the gems are just barely behind the next strike of the pick-axe. The one who doesn't give up and keeps chopping away will reap the reward. It's the agent who stays consistent in chipping away the dirt that finds the gems. Quit trying to avoid the hard work.

Zillow also keeps changing the game. First, they wanted to sell zip codes to agents for a low monthly fee. They weren't making money that way, so they decided to go after the top producers who could afford to pay a $3,000 per month fee, which cuts out the little guys whose pockets aren't that deep. Zillow continuously has to keep recruiting new people willing to pay the fee.

Remember, Zillow is marketing to a group of people with a nearly 90 percent career failure rate within their first two years. Not a very sustainable model.

If you're going to make it in this business, you will have to deal with actual, live people. There's just no way around it. While a platform like Facebook is a decent way to get the conversation started about your new real estate business, it's still not any better than picking up a telephone and talking to a live person. People will always remember that phone call much better than a post on social media. There's a very well-known tire company in Tulsa and its surrounding suburban cities that has been led by a man for over fifty years. He also happens to host a men's lunch and networking meeting every month. He makes over one hundred phone calls to personally invite people each month! Not only is the turnout better because he's able to make the calls, but the thing that separates him from the other luncheons and networking events is the personal touch of a phone call. Person-to-person really does work!

Your version of person-to-person includes networking and leads; these are priorities and skills you can learn. There's simply no quick way around it. Once you determine to make these a priority, your confidence will grow and so will your business.

Action: Be a chief referrer. Build relationships with referral partners whose businesses are related to homes (i.e. plumbers, electricians, etc). Refer business to them and they will refer to you.

CHAPTER 5

Training vs. Education

*"Real estate is the key cost of physical retailers.
That's why there's the old saying: location, location,
location."*

-Jeff Bezos

This section is the heart of what I believe makes all the difference in the world for a new agent's success. There is a difference between training and education.

I'm going to make a crude analogy to make this point stick. Let's say I have a beautiful daughter who comes home from school and says, "Hey Dad, the school is offering two sex education courses to choose from next month. I can either enroll in the education class where we'll watch videos and discuss questions with the school nurse, or I can enroll in the hands-on training class where we'll go on dates with guys and practice sexual moves in his back seat." See! There is a major difference between training and education!

Education is not a bad thing, especially if your daughter is involved (in fact, education should be 100 percent of the learning method in the above example). However, when it comes to the real estate business, hands-on training should be the majority of your learning. The best way to learn the business is by going into the field with an agent who understands how to train you. If you want to learn how to work an open house, you need to go along with a mentor and watch closely what they do and say during the open house.

By receiving hands-on training, you will learn most of what you need to know to be successful. And it's more impactful to be shown how to do something. On the flip side, when an agent trains someone, they benefit too since you retain more of what you teach. What a beautiful system!

Mentoring and teaching someone requires skill too. It's not always automatic. I have recruited very high-producing agents over the years. I've learned that even they can use help at times when it comes to showing other agents how to succeed. Here's what I mean. I hired a top real estate agent that wanted to build a team. I told him that first we were going to do three open houses together so he could learn the system. He told me he was a rockstar at open houses, but agreed to let me come with him. As I watched him talk to potential buyers, I heard him say things like, "I've sold more houses in this neighborhood in the last year than any other agent," and "I've negotiated over eighty transactions in the last year." These things were all true for him, but are not statistics a new agent can use.

So, what information does a new agent have that they can use at their first open house? Saying, "I have no idea what I'm doing and probably will not be much help, but hey, you should use me to find your next home," won't be very effective. I explained to the agent at the open houses that if he wants to build a business, he would have to make what he says duplicatable. That's the only way to build hundreds of agents in a short time.

"Great Steve-O, now what do I do with this information? Should I just go ask my broker to train me?" Let's look at the typical life of a broker who owns a firm with over one hundred agents. Their job is to constantly recruit more agents to combat agent turnover in the office. They also are making themselves available for calls from their agents at all times of the day, sometimes taking four calls a day from a single new agent who just needs help with minor questions. Now multiply that by one hundred agents. You can see why most brokers just don't have time to take a new agent into the field for hands-on training.

But, imagine if that same broker has one hundred well-trained agents who are capable of training the new agents. The agents will all benefit! Whether you've had one contract or one hundred contracts, the learning does not stop. This is a form of "servant-leadership"—the person who leads becomes the one who serves to teach, and that person becomes the leader who becomes the server … and so on. It really is a beautiful way to build a person, not just a business.

There is a reason you see so many small real estate brokerage firms. Many high-producing agents started in large firms and realized that they taught themselves the business. Because of this, they see no reason to keep paying the broker, who is no longer providing them with anything they can't do on their own. So, they become a broker and add teammates.

If you are in a firm with less than ten agents in the office, it's pretty tough to make any money. This is because the broker running that team often is also competing for sales. Because they are still in the business, they are still trying to make sales and don't have time to mentor you. The other thing to be aware of is that they will be a hard act to follow. Chances are that you're not going to be able to duplicate their style of doing business. Learning to do business in a way that works for you, ultimately tailoring it to fit your personality, is the best way. It takes time, but it works.

Action: Preview many houses, especially looking for things that are not shown in photos.

CHAPTER 6

Don't Stop. Keep Believing.

*"Success in real estate comes down to two factors:
taking care of and valuing the customer."*

- Michael Miedler

"The buck stops here." That phrase was made popular in the late 1940s by President Harry S. Truman. He kept a sign with that phrase on his desk in the Oval Office. As an entrepreneur and business owner, I have no doubt of the meaning of that saying! When you are the leader, and everyone depends on you for their livelihood, you don't pass the responsibility to someone else. As the leader of Kevo, I knew everyone was looking at me for leadership and how to make it in real estate. I knew it would be very important to remind them never to give up and to show, by my example, to keep believing and never to stop. I learned this lesson through some of the most difficult times in my life.

In addition to building Kevo Properties, I was a dad and husband. As an entrepreneur or business owner, it's neverending.

By this time, my wife and I had completely liquidated our savings and we had eighteen agents as part of Kevo. Throughout the second year, Brandi was basically supporting us both with her jobs at the salon. Toward the end of that year, she went to the doctor for a routine checkup. They found a lump in her breast. She had a biopsy and was diagnosed with Stage 3 breast cancer. As far as statistics go, one out of eight women is diagnosed with breast cancer every year. When you or someone you love is "the one," it changes so much. She immediately started treatment, which turned into a grueling three-year process.

Sometimes we hear so much about cancer it seems common. But these are real people battling for their lives. For Brandi, those three years included surgeries, chemotherapy, and radiation. I remember Brandi combing her hair one day and gigantic amounts of it came out. She ended up going to the salon and one of her friends shaved her head. We were still a new couple, and this was really hard on her emotionally. But even through all of the pain and the emotional roller-coaster, she stayed strong and kept fighting. She always found a way to keep going, and the kids hardly even realized she was sick. With four kids, wigs, and her spiritual grounding, she made it through and is more beautiful today than ever.

About a year and a half into her treatment, chemotherapy and radiation were almost burning her skin off, so we agreed she had to quit working at the salon. She gave up her business after eighteen years. I remember thinking we were just going to have to find a way to do this financially. One of the things I always worried about was our health insurance. Since I left Hobby Lobby, we were no longer on a big group plan. We were now on an individual plan with an extremely high deductible of $10,000 per person.

Just when I thought things couldn't get worse, they did. In the middle of her treatment, our son, Talan, was in a sledding accident. He came down a hill and hit his face on a T-post. It split his mouth so badly he required plastic surgery. Now on top of ongoing chemotherapy and radiation bills, we were hit with a $27,000 plastic surgery bill. Thankfully the surgeon was successful, and our son would be fine.

I'm sharing all these personal moments from our past because I want to remind you that no one is immune to storms. Everyone has faced them and will again at some point. In Oklahoma, we have winter, spring, summer, fall, and an additional season—"storm season." Some "storm seasons" are short, and some are longer. However, the good news is that they do end. There is always an appointed time for a storm to end, even though we can't forecast it. The same is true with our lives. Storms will come, but they will go too. My life was no different. The storms my family endured taught me so much about my faith and how to navigate my world.

Another reason I'm sharing is to take away excuses. When life is hard personally or professionally, sometimes those moments can give us a reason to quit. Some quit whatever profession they're in and use the storms of life as an excuse as to why they failed. Some quit life. They check-out mentally, emotionally, spiritually, or physically. I had every opportunity to quit in every way. But where would I be now?

One of the biggest storms of my life personally had been raging for several years, and about the time it seemed to be over, the waves crashed once again. My oldest son had been a heroin addict for five years. The addiction caused him to contract a disease that was essentially eating his heart, and he was admitted to the hospital. It finally got to the point where he had so many holes in his heart that he needed a heart transplant. He was given the gift of life when we were informed he would be receiving a new heart. I stayed with him throughout the entire surgery process, sleeping there every night. He miraculously came through the surgery and everything seemed great.

When he was admitted to the hospital, he weighed 160 pounds. He gained one hundred pounds in water weight while he was there. Just five days post-surgery, the hospital released him to go home. His skin looked like it was going to explode because of the water weight, and he still had to have IV antibiotics. His mother didn't want to take him to her house, so Brandi insisted he stay with us and our other three children.

Over the next three months, he stayed with me 24/7, lost all the water weight, and recovered. He had a dynamic personality and looked great. He came to the office with me at Kevo working at the front desk. One day out of the blue, he told me there was a job opening at the Arby's headquarters right around the corner in the same complex. It was 4:00 p.m., and he was going to walk over there to apply. An hour passed and I was still waiting for him to come back. Then another hour passed. I knew in my heart after the first hour when he didn't return that he had run off, that he was gone. It was a sickening feeling.

I didn't hear from him for forty-five days until I received a call from the county jail. He had collapsed while incarcerated and had been taken back to the hospital. He had re-contracted the same disease as before, only now with his new, transplanted heart.

36

Addiction … It's not a new topic in our country, unfortunately. Opioids take the life of close to 128 people a day (as of 2018 according to the www.drugabuse.gov website). When we hear statistics like that it's easy to become complacent, unless your child or someone you love is one of those 128. Opioids is a large class of drugs causing the overdoses, which includes heroin, my son's nemesis. Heroin is made from morphine and is highly addictive. If you've never dealt with drug addiction in your family, it's time to pause and be grateful to God. It seemed God continued to give my son chances at life. Miraculously, he received a second heart transplant, all within a three-month span. Again, he made it through the surgery without complications.

Sadly, I found out that while he was recovering from the second heart transplant, his friends were sneaking into the hospital and shooting him up with heroin. The hospital started moving him from room to room, trying to hide him from his friends. I went up to see him one afternoon. As I walked into his room, I knew someone was hiding in the bathroom. It was just a parent's "sixth sense." I thought, "You know, he wants to die." I decided right then I wasn't going to watch it. I told him I loved him, left the hospital, and never went back. He died in the hospital shortly after that.

To this day, I don't know how anybody gets through something like that. I don't know how I got through it. But I got to the point where I felt that I didn't have a choice. I had to keep going. We had about forty agents by then, and when you're leading a team, you can't go into the office depressed or sad. It's not that you don't feel the sadness inside, but you have to choose a different direction for your thoughts. You have to consciously take each thought captive (2 Corinthians 10:5). If all I did was focus on how I was feeling and how sad the entire situation was, my thoughts would have consumed me. My work would have declined and anyone working with me would have felt it. Ultimately, my company would have deteriorated and likely failed. Have you ever walked into a home and you automatically know the people in there had just been arguing? Yes! We all have! Well, in the same way, depression is contagious, but so is joy. I know that may sound too simple, but it's true. If you smile at someone, the majority of the time they will smile back, whether you know them or not. Leading a team of professionals, I knew this was critical. I had to be upbeat, positive, and encouraging, both at work and at home. Everything I could possibly think of that I didn't want to happen to me was dumped on top of me. I just knew there were no options, I couldn't quit.

It was November and right before Thanksgiving. Coleman, our thirteen-year-old, was feeling sick and said he wasn't very hungry. We recognized he had lost about thirty-five pounds over four months, but assumed he was just growing and we had changed our entire household over to a healthier organic diet. Before this rapid weight loss, Coleman needed to lose some weight, as we all did. We thought our new diet was the reason he was losing as much weight as he was. He was drinking more water than ever, but still eating and very active. He was so sick the morning I took him to the doctor and after several tests they diagnosed the reason as Type 1 Diabetes. "Holy smokes, please not one more thing!!!"

We learned to adjust within the family, and, hoping to understand and have everyone involved, we thought if everyone pricked their fingers to see what their own blood sugar levels were, then Coleman would know we were all in and with him through trying to understand. The next two months were not easy.

One night around 10:00 p.m., the upstairs floor was shaking like an earthquake was happening (we did live in a 1930s house, so we heard everything). We then heard our older son, Ethan, scream, "Help, it's Coleman." Coleman was having his very first seizure. We called the ambulance because we didn't even have the EpiPen to shoot him with. This scared all of us to death, especially Ethan. Sadly, this was not to be his last one. Nope!

Brandi and I left early one morning about a week later leaving

Ethan and Coleman at home alone. They were still asleep, so we thought surely we could be back before they would be up on Saturday morning. We left by 8:00 a.m., but by 10:00 a.m. Coleman woke up not feeling well, and Ethan was eating a bowl of cereal. Coleman looked at Ethan and said he wasn't feeling so good and then collapsed onto the floor in our kitchen. Thankfully this time Ethan was ready; he grabbed the EpiPen, and, with no hesitation, stabbed him in the leg. Ethan, only fifteen at the time, was so brave and yet scared. We walked in and they were still on the floor. We did panic, but we were glad Ethan had been there. There is always that "What If?" Over the years, less of these occurrences happened, mostly because Coleman started to realize he was the only one that could own his own health and now as an adult is doing very well.

Action: Capture your thoughts that are not healthy. Don't judge them in the moment.

CHAPTER 7

The Edge ... Mental Toughness

"I will forever believe that buying a home is a great investment. Why? Because you can't live in a stock certificate. You can't live in a mutual fund."

- Oprah Winfrey

For the longest time, I lived with my phone attached to my ear. Agents were constantly calling with questions: "How do you do this?" and "How do you do that?" This went on every night easily up until 9:00 p.m.-10:00 p.m. Brandi would say, "Why do they keep calling? Don't they know how to do their job?" But the thing was, I couldn't not pick up the phone to answer their questions, and the agent who happened to be calling didn't know that there were also ten other agents calling me with the same or similar questions. I also knew that it wouldn't last forever, or at least that's what I told Brandi in those early days. I knew if I was going to do this the way it should be done, it wouldn't be only me doing the training. The idea was to train others to do what I was doing and duplicate the success.

When you're the owner of a business, you work with all kinds of people. Some you like and some you don't. In the second year of Kevo, I had an agent come work for me who had an overly annoying personality. Everybody was annoyed with her – from the office staff to fellow agents, even her own clients. However, she did the job. She was always around doing the right things and got fifteen listings in ninety days. She was following my system. . . . It will work for anyone. However, I ended up closing on all of them because by that time her clients didn't want her coming around anymore.

I had multiple people ask me why I put up with her or why I would stop and listen to her. When you were as financially wrecked as I was initially and you have somebody willing to put in the work and stay with you, it changes the way you look at people. You learned to appreciate certain qualities and ignore the bad ones (besides, she made us $15,000 a year).

When you've seen a REALTOR® pull up to a house in a new vehicle, and they walk in the house wearing business attire, looking like they just stepped out of a salon, it can give the illusion that's all you need in order to have total confidence in this business. Some people think they're going to mentally wake up one day and suddenly have complete confidence, nothing will scare them, or they're not going to have any doubt. That's a complete myth! It's all about controlling the fears and doubts and learning to become confident in spite of those feelings. Here's what I mean: When people start out calling "For Sale by Owners," it's intimidating and scary. If I had to do that today, I still wouldn't like it. You're not going to get to the point where you like it. When you're doing things that are uncomfortable, you're never going to wake up and say, "I love doing this!" It's a lie. If you're normal, you'll never get over those feelings.

You learn to push yourself mentally to say, "This is just how it is." The only time you're winning is when you're out of your comfort zone. I wake up almost every day doubting something I did or something I'm doing. But you have to realize that doing nothing is worse! You can't just dip your toe in; you have to jump right into the deep end without a net. You need to fight your way through knowing you're going to make mistakes. Along the way, though, you realize as long as you have the ability to make another decision to correct that mistake, you're fine. Making decisions and moving forward is the only way to go.

You have to get yourself mentally ready. A friend of mine used to prepare her son for a shot by telling him the truth, "It's going to hurt a little bit, but it's to help you feel better faster. And if it hurts, it will be over faster than you can take three deep breaths. When we're done, we'll do something fun!" It worked for him. Why do we work so hard to avoid pain? This same woman used this idea to talk with her son because of her personal experience with shots. When she had one as a little girl, her parents told her it wouldn't hurt. So, when it did, she was determined to avoid ever getting a shot again. When she had an infection from a cut on her leg, she avoided telling her parents because she didn't want a shot. It got to the point she was limping so bad that her parents finally asked what in the world was going on. And not only did she end up getting a shot, but she got three of them! All to avoid the pain.

We work too hard to avoid pain that can help us! When you get past the thought that you may not like it, deal with that and stop looking for an easier way out. Your thoughts can kill you;

they'll make you or break you. Your brain has one purpose, and that is to protect you from pain. It goes into self-defense mode and wants to shut down. It's designed to protect you. If you touch something that's too hot, your brain tells you to pull back; if something is uncomfortable, you don't want to do it; if something is too high, you move away before you fall. That's what your brain does. The battle between success and failure is fought inside your brain that is trying to protect you from being uncomfortable.

Of all the hurdles I had to overcome in building Kevo Properties, one caught me unprepared ... loneliness. When you're on your own and have to make every decision, they don't affect anybody other than yourself. When you become a leader, you're able to delegate and make fewer decisions. But the ones you do make have more of an impact. It's no longer just about you. It can feel isolating and takes more of an effort to intentionally connect with people that have nothing to do with business.

We have around 350 agents today and are growing. If I make a bad call, it doesn't just impact me. Any decision I make now affects 350 people, their families, their livelihood, and the direction for their future. The weird part about loneliness is I'm surrounded by people; I have business coaches, spiritual coaches, my wife, and other REALTORS®. I can get guidance and counsel from all of them, but ultimately, it's up to me alone to make the decision. No one can make it for me.

If I went to the agents for advice, even the ones that have been with me a long time, I would still have to decide on my own. They don't know all the intricacies involved. They only know a portion of what's going on within Kevo. In the end, they wouldn't be completely truthful with me anyway. It's human nature or self-preservation or whatever you want to call it. They're not going to go against me because I'm the boss.

There's a reason they don't build monuments to committees (I'm not saying I want a monument, that's the last thing I'd want). I'm trying to illustrate that if you choose to lead and be a leader, it's going to be very lonely at the top. This is especially true anytime there's a big decision to be made.

Not only is it lonely being a leader, but it's also lonely for the agent. When you start as a new agent, you get out of school and quickly realize this is entirely a self-development program. It's really about the agent. You have to learn to become more attractive to more people in order to be successful. Your wife can't do it for you. Your husband can't do it for you.

The only way you do this is to become more knowledgeable and work on yourself. It's not about working with the public. It is not about working with your team. The only thing that will make you better is you working on yourself. That's why it's a lonely business. You have to fix yourself, and you'll be doing it by yourself. You are the problem and the solution.

I've watched many people throughout the years who have said they want to go out on their own, start their own business. Financially, some of them do it the way I did when I started Kevo; I took my savings and thought that would keep me going. Others have used their retirement, thinking it was the perfect time since they have a cushion. However, most of them don't do anything until that cushion runs out. Because of this, anytime somebody told me they wanted to quit their job to start their own business, I would try to talk them out of it. I'd tell them to wait until they had saved up enough money.

But over the years, my advice has changed. I've learned you need to be under financial pressure in order to do the work that needs to be done to be successful, especially starting out. If you're being stretched financially, you're either going to cave in and get out, or you're going to buckle down and do what needs to be done. That will prove whether or not you're an entrepreneur. A woman from Oklahoma owns a multi-billion dollar cosmetic company. She tells the story of the advice her stepdad, who was an executive with the company she was working for at the time, gave her when she decided to launch out and go for her dream. Her dream was to own her own cosmetic company. She sought her stepdad's advice on whether to quit her well-paying job to begin her own company or keep that job and wait until she established her new company before she quit. Her stepfather told her to quit her job and "burn the bridge." He told her that if she knew she could still work, or could go back to her old job if it didn't work out, she wouldn't and couldn't be "all-in." So she did just that, she quit. She built a multi-billion dollar cosmetic empire mainly based on one product, and has women worldwide selling her products. It worked for her, it worked for me, and it's the only way it will work for you. So, from now on, if somebody asks when they should start, I say "Now!"

Growing up, your parents took care of you, both physically and financially. You probably didn't have to worry about anything. When you went to college, you took care of yourself physically, but many of your parents were still paying for you. Let's say you got married and thought you were finally financially independent. Not really independent, because 95 percent of you had jobs. This means you were still being taken care of by somebody else, an entrepreneur. That's why I tell people that if they want to be truly independent, they need to just take the leap and start now. Entrepreneurs are the only ones who take care of themselves.

There's a huge difference between education and experience. I believe in education, and it's necessary for many, just not for everyone. You can go to school, read everything you can get your hands on, or do all the online studying in the world. But until you actually go out and do the job, it doesn't mean anything. Actual experience is what creates knowledge. There is no education, nothing at all really, that can take the place of experience.

Vince Lombardi, legendary coach of the Green Bay Packers, held up a football on the first day of training camp in 1961 and said, "Gentlemen, this is a football." He was trying to make the point that it's the basics that matter, and he was absolutely right. A lot of new agents want to skip over the basics. They'll come to me when they're just starting out and ask me to teach them the "ninja stuff." There is no ninja stuff!

It's all about the basics. It's about showing up every day and doing the little things. But the reason people want to abandon the basics is because it's boring. I can tell you three things to do for your entire career and that's all you'll ever need. But nobody wants to hear that. They all think there has to be some kind of ninja move. There isn't a ninja move. You actually become a ninja by mastering the boring, little stuff.

Action: Search for a video of someone you admire and watch it.

CHAPTER 8

I Got Schooled

"Successful people do what unsuccessful people are not willing to do. Don't wish it were easier; wish you were better."

-Jim Rohn

If you've ever thought you have to be extremely smart to be successful, I think I can disprove that theory in just a few minutes. Looking back, kindergarten was the only grade I really nailed. I completely aced it for a couple of reasons: 1.) It involved blocks, playing, and lunch pails, and 2.) There were sleep mats and nap times, and I loved naps. Every day, I'd wake up drooling from my nap. I thought Mrs. Johnson was a great teacher, and that grade level was my one success story for many, many years.

Once I got past kindergarten, my whole world started changing in a very negative way. For some reason, I was terrified to go to school in first grade. I don't know if I even knew why at the time, and I still don't really have an explanation for it. Whenever my parents asked me what was wrong or what was going on, I couldn't answer them. As I said, I don't know if I even had an answer.

I was really struggling, and this wasn't normal for me. For about two weeks, every morning was an absolute battle. I went crazy in the mornings, screaming, crying, and throwing fit after fit. I didn't usually throw fits. I wasn't a child who had temper tantrums all the time. Up until then, I was a pretty happy kid. But something changed that school year. My mom didn't have a driver's license until I got mine when I was sixteen, so my dad drove me to school. He would literally have to drag me out of the house to get me into the car in the mornings. Once we made it to school and he finally got me into the classroom and left, that's when the true terror would begin for me.

About two weeks into the school year, I remember it all came to a head one day in the classroom. The teacher (I think I blocked her name from my memory also) wanted me to move. I can't remember if she wanted me to go out of the room or just go somewhere else inside the class. Regardless, what I do remember is what happened. I grabbed onto my desk and refused to move. I couldn't move. It was like I was paralyzed.

The teacher kept insisting I move, and when I refused, she grabbed my arms, trying to pull my hands loose. I remember she pulled and pulled, but my grip on the desk was too strong.

Finally, when she couldn't get my hands loose, she slapped me across the face to get me to let go. Once I did let go, she proceeded to grab my arm and marched me to the principal's office. The principal ended up sending me to the counselor's office.

For the next six months, I spent every school day in the counselor's office talking with the counselor. I don't remember if I even went out to recess or not, but I know I wasn't in the classroom for the whole day. And here's the crazy part. My parents didn't know I was going there. They didn't know that I was spending all day, every day talking to the counselor while she tried to figure out what was the psychological problem. All my parents knew was that all of a sudden, it was easy to get me to go to school. Overnight, my crazy fits in the mornings stopped and I became completely compliant.

Somehow my parents finally figured out what was going on. They found out about the incident in the classroom that started the whole thing. Immediately, they went up to the school. The teacher that slapped me was fired. The counselor was also fired for not notifying my parents about what was going on every day. Then I was sent back to a regular classroom where Mrs. Cochran became my first-grade teacher.

Obviously, I was "held back" that year and had to repeat the first grade. That meant from that point on, I was always the oldest student in my class. I realize it's more common now for kids to be held back and that the reasons vary. This familiarity has helped cut out the stigma that used to go with it. When I was held back, I thought it was because I was stupid. I was completely insecure and even the simplest tasks were difficult, if not impossible for me. Just reading a page or two was overwhelming because I couldn't remember the content from the previous page. Nothing made sense to me. Even the thought of going into a classroom was daunting.

Even now, I remember what school smells like. School buildings have a weird smell. Many adults feel a sense of nostalgia when they walk into their old school and think of the "good old days," but not me. Every time I go to a school with my kids, even to this day, I immediately recognize the smell, and the feelings associated with it come back. As soon as I walk in, I feel those same insecure feelings assaulting me. It doesn't last very long, but it's still there.

Knowing internally that something was wrong with me in school, I knew I had to do something. If I couldn't study hard enough or if I had some kind of learning disability, I decided I had to figure out a way to hide it. I don't know that I consciously thought about it when I first began, but I started hiding everything. I started developing different strategies to make school easier for me and to hide my insecurities. The way I was able to survive school was my "strategies for success."

By the time I got to fifth grade, I had perfected the "Teacher's Pet Strategy." I realized that if I hung out with the teacher and did all the chores like cleaning the erasers, it made it easier for me. If I showed I was willing to help out and actually be happy doing it, that made it even better. I'd end up getting a little bit of extra favor from the teacher. They weren't quite as hard on me.

I remember Mrs. Hefner from fifth grade. During class, she would walk around observing the students' work. I don't recall what subject we were working on at the time, but Mrs. Hefner stopped beside my desk. After seeing my answers, she reached down with her finger and actually pointed at one of the problems for me to check. So, the "Teacher's Pet Strategy" was a success. I was able to hide the fact that I didn't understand any subject.

In middle school and going into high school, I perfected the "Friends and Girlfriends Strategy." I realized most kids in school would give you the answers if you just asked. I don't know why they did this. I suspect it's partly because it made them feel smarter. Whatever the reason, I got into the habit of finding out which of my friends were good in each of my subjects. I'd then go to them and get answers to homework. I'd get help on projects. I'd go to whatever girlfriend I had at the time and, depending on how smart she was, have her do my writing assignments for me. I was almost never turned down, so this strategy worked great too!

Going into middle school, I started realizing that everybody was good in at least one subject. I had friends who excelled in algebra, but maybe didn't get quite as good grades in English. I had other friends who did great in science, but didn't do as well in history. The only subject I excelled at was P.E. Other than that, I wasn't good in any of the core subjects. And when I say not good, I mean I struggled to get D's. I honestly think some of my teachers gave me a D instead of an F just because they wanted me out of their classroom. I desperately wanted to be ordinary when it came to my grades. You know how people will say about someone who commits a crime, "If they worked as hard at a regular job as they did to sell dope, they'd be a success." I'm sure people would have said that about me if they would have known how much time I spent perfecting all these "strategies" to just barely get by. It wasn't going to let them know, so I kept having to figure out how to hide.

I also developed a strategy to keep others from seeing my grades, to hide how poorly I was doing. I call it the "Paper Placement Strategy." Teachers would pass out papers with your grade written, usually in red ink, on the top right corner. My paper always had a giant red D or F. When the teacher would lay your paper down, the three or four people around you were going to look at it and compare their grade. I had to figure out a way to cover my grade quickly without looking like that's what I was doing. I didn't even want to see my grade and I certainly didn't want others seeing it! I came up with an ingenious strategy. I would stretch my arms out right before I knew the teacher was going to pass out grades. I'd hold my pencil and lean way over the top of my desk, doing a giant stretch. I'd wait for the teacher to get right up to my desk, then I would lift my arm. The teacher would place the paper on my desk, and I'd quickly put my arm back down and continue my stretch. I know that seems like a lot of effort to cover up my grade, but I learned how to do it quickly. I knew all the kids around me would be looking at their own grade first for a few seconds. My goal then was to cover mine before anyone looked around. I became an expert at this, and it worked perfectly every time.

After all these years, I still remember these strategies vividly and even the feelings I would have during the time.

Another effective tactic I used was the "Back Corner Strategy." This strategy helped with hiding in two different ways. First, you could literally hide. I found out the harder it was for a teacher to see you, the less they called on you. By sitting in the very back corner, the teacher had a harder time noticing you, especially if you stayed quiet and slouched down in your chair a little. Second, this strategy also helped in hiding your grades. When you're sitting in the back corner, there are less people who even have the opportunity to see your grade. This made it easier to hide it when papers were handed out. Besides, most kids who sat in the back were like me; they also didn't want to be noticed and tended to mind their own business.

Finally, in high school, I employed the "Flattery and Flirt Strategy." Keep in mind there were a lot of newer, younger teachers at my school. We're talking maybe twenty-three- and twenty-four-year-olds. Now remember, I was the oldest one in the group, seventeen or eighteen years old at the time. What I did was find the teachers you could tell liked the attention they received from high school guys. They were flattered which also helped to distract them. I would then pick my teachers based on this. (I feel like I need to point out here that nothing inappropriate ever happened between myself and any of my teachers.) However, I discovered that if I flirted a little and gave them compliments here and there, they were much more forgiving on my paperwork. Instead of getting a D like I deserved, I might have gotten a C instead.

I never asked any of my teachers for help. I never went to my parents and told them what was going on. Besides, my parents didn't expect much out of me other than just to pass. Therefore, my goal in every class was to get through it with a passing grade without anybody realizing how illiterate I really was. I recall I had to take algebra four times before I finally passed with a D. I still didn't understand any of it, and I'm sure I cheated my way through it.

Tenth grade marked a changing point in my life. That was

when everything turned around for me. I was introduced to Mrs. Clara Luper, the civil rights activist from the 1950s. She led the Oklahoma City sit-in movement, where she and others conducted sit-in protests of drugstore lunch counters. This led to the overturn of their segregation policies. Mrs. Luper was also a schoolteacher, and in tenth grade, she taught my history and debate class.

From the very beginning, I was fascinated with both her and her classroom. For the first time, I started to excel at something in school. Something unique happened during all the work I put in forming all my different strategies; I started figuring out how people operate. I also liked to talk. Because of this, I did really well in debate. It came easy to me. And if you're debating and doing it well, everybody else could see you're good at something. My confidence began to grow for the first time ever in school.

At the same time, I also discovered the cool part about history. Mrs. Luper showed us that history is mostly made up of stories. I could remember stories, so I began to excel in that class, also. I started receiving grades I was actually proud of. I finally got grades I didn't have to try and hide.

To this day, I'm not the best speller. I couldn't spell my way out of a wet paper sack. I used to hide it, but I don't anymore. I'm open about it. I can't even use spell check on my phone because half of the time I can't get close enough to the word for it to work. I have to read daily to stay sharp, but mostly in short paragraph form. I found out I'm a paragraphs and headlines reader.

Having Clara Luper as a teacher was a major turning point in my life. That's when everything started to change for me. Looking back, she is the person who helped me believe in myself. She's the one who taught me that there was something I could excel in, and I just needed to focus on that. And because I was finally excelling at something, I went from being a hiding introvert to actually stepping out and trying new things.

That's how I know you don't have to be extremely smart to be successful. The key to success has nothing to do with whether or not you're good at algebra, English, or science; what it really comes down to is figuring out what you enjoy doing, what you like, what you're passionate about. I was blessed to have a teacher who saw something in me which helped me to see it in myself. It's part of who I am now, and my mission involves helping others to be able to do that for themselves.

Action: Be transparent enough to get the help that you need.

CHAPTER 9

Your Belief System

"Owning a home is a keystone of wealth—both financial affluence and emotional security."

- Suze Orman

Ask yourself, "Why do I do what I do?" You need to consider the influences in your life and why they're so important. Everybody operates based on their own personal belief system which is formed when you are young. Your personal belief system is influenced by your experiences, and the people you come into contact with throughout your life. This impacts every decision you make. I still make decisions every day based on the belief system that was formed from bits and pieces of other people. Looking back, four different people influenced me so greatly, it accounts for about 90 percent of how I operate today. Allow me to introduce them to you and what I learned from them.

MY DAD

The person that has had the biggest impact on my life, both personally and professionally, is my dad, Roger. My dad is seventy-six years old, and because of him I don't miss work. My dad never missed work when I was growing up. He just kept going no matter how sick he was. I can't remember ever seeing my dad home in bed, ever.

I recall the time my dad came down with the mumps. There aren't many people who get the mumps today because of vaccinations, so you may not be familiar with how the disease works. Most people don't know what this old timey disease is—there is a vaccine now. According to www.mayoclinic.org, "Mumps is a viral infection that primarily affects saliva-producing (salivary) glands that are located near your ears. Mumps can cause swelling in one or both of these glands." Many times, someone would have "chipmunk cheeks" from the swelling. Also, symptoms included fever, fatigue, loss of appetite, and other symptoms that could intensify. My dad refused to stay home from work. Because he was moving around so much, his symptoms intensified and spread into his chest. Even with this, he continued going to work and didn't miss a single day.

That really stuck with me. To this day, I just don't miss work. I can't help it. When I was in my forties, I was working for Hobby Lobby. I had five hundred employees that worked in the warehouse underneath me. In the winter, we would occasionally have snowstorms, and of course, I always went in. Not long after getting there, managers would start calling the warehouse asking if it was going to be open that day. I would always ask them, "Why did you call here?" Well, I already knew the answer to that question. They called the warehouse because they knew I'd be there. Even though they weren't there, they just accepted that I would be. That work ethic came from my dad.

Another thing my dad taught me was to never quit working and striving for more. My dad was always trying to make more money. He was constantly coming up with new ideas and new things to build in order to support the family. He was always working on a project, the next big thing.

One of his money-making ventures was roll bars for the back of four-wheel drive trucks. He built roll bars, put big lights on top, and sold them. It's funny because back then I thought the purpose of a roll bar was to use after a high school baseball or football game. My friends and I would all jump into the back of my dad's truck. He would go fifty miles per hour with all of us standing in the back holding onto the roll bar. Can you imagine today if you saw a truck driving on the street with ten kids standing in the back? People go crazy if they see a dog back there now, but no one thought twice about all of us standing back there when I was younger!

Watching my dad build things was hilarious. He was a one-man operator and always worked on his projects at our house. The only time he ever asked for help was when he'd have my mom, my brothers, or myself hold up pieces while he worked. One day he was building motorcycle trailers, and my mom got the task of holding up pieces while he welded. She was wearing bell-bottom jeans, which tells you what year that might have been. The next thing you know, my dad had caught the bottom of her pants on fire! She was running around the yard, grabbing the water hose to put the fire out! It was like an episode of "America's Funniest Home Videos" played out right in front of me! (Thankfully, she was fine.)

The final project my dad attempted was the only time my mom

ever said, "No." This was unusual. She was always supportive of my dad and everything he did, but this was the one time she put her foot down. At a garage sale, my dad found a one-person helicopter that was in pretty bad shape. Of course, he bought it, threw it in the back of his truck, and brought it home. His plan was to put this tiny little thing together and try to launch it. If you knew my dad, you'd know he was always pretty good at everything he did, but the one thing he never worried about was safety.

When we were younger, my brothers and I had a little motorcycle that my dad rebuilt. The only problem was it didn't have brakes on it! My dad let us ride it anyways! Our brake system was that you better be able to turn or put your foot down like Fred Flintstone to stop it. Because of this and other "safety" issues in the past, my mom refused to let my dad work on the helicopter, even though he bought it.

Growing up, my dad was continually moving on from thing to thing, one money-making project after another. This probably explains why in my early years of trying to be an entrepreneur, I jumped from one thing to the next. I didn't realize you have to stick with something for more than just one project. In reality, you have to do something for almost ten years before it really pays off. Some may see that as a negative thing my dad taught me, but I see it as a positive. From his example, I eventually learned to quit jumping around, and instead work hard on perfecting one thing.

I also learned how to be a husband and father from my dad. He treated my mother with love and respect and always put her first. He set the mark and showed me how I should treat my own wife. Growing up, my dad was fun and tremendously funny. He attended all of our games, no matter the sport. He always supported us and told us we could accomplish anything and be anything we wanted to be. That's what I hope I've passed on to my own children.

MRS. CLARA LUPER

My next great inspiration and hero was Mrs. Clara Luper. Although she's mentioned earlier, this woman is certainly valuable enough in my life to bring to this part of the book too. Clara Luper is somewhat famous, especially in Oklahoma. In Oklahoma City, there is a streetscape and civic beautification project close to the state capital named the Clara Luper Corridor. Also, Oklahoma City public schools named the district's administrative offices the Clara Luper Center for Educational Services. As I mentioned before, I had the privilege of having Mrs. Luper as my tenth-grade history teacher at John Marshall High School in Oklahoma City. However, she was a civil rights activist before she became my teacher.

As I referenced previously, Clara Luper led the Oklahoma City sit-in movement in the 1950s. It started in 1958 when she led about eighty African-Americans, including her young daughter and son, several of her students, and others into the segregated Katz Drug Store in downtown Oklahoma City. They sat at the lunch counter and asked to be served. They were refused service and the police were called. The group wasn't arrested, and they stayed there from the time the store opened until they closed, returning the following day. Two days after the sit-in began, Katz desegregated its lunch counters in three states. Although she wasn't arrested that time, I think she said she'd been arrested twenty-seven times.

She was done being arrested by the time she was my teacher, and she taught me many invaluable lessons. If your memory is strong enough then you can debate. Clara saw this in me.

She encouraged me and pushed me to get onto a stage in front of the entire school. I only actually spoke for ten seconds. But those ten seconds launched me into a career of a lot of public speaking. I learned how to debate in her classroom. We were always doing mock trials in her class, and through that, I thrived. I had been such a huge introvert, and that got me out of my box. It showed me that I was able to stand up and succeed at something.

Additionally, our class was doing a short little play in front of the student body, and she wanted me to participate. It was only ten words, but of course, I didn't want to do it. She made me feel confident that I could and this gave me the courage to do it. Speaking those ten words in front of 350 people changed me. I was able to conquer my fear of speaking in front of groups and I've used this skill countless times in my business. And that's all because of her getting me outside my comfort zone.

I recall a true story she told in class one day. Somehow a rumor got started that she was going to buy a house in one of the most exclusive and expensive neighborhoods in Oklahoma City called Nichols Hills. She laughed and told us, "I couldn't have even afforded the electric bill in a house that big!" In typical Clara Luper style, she jumped in her car and drove to the neighborhood. She pulled up in front of the property and got out of her car with a legal pad. With that note pad she walked around, taking notes. All the while, she looked like she was a buyer for the property. Some of the neighbors were peeking out their windows watching what was happening. After doing this for several minutes, she got back in her car and left. Apparently, the thought of an African American moving into the neighborhood scared the neighbors so badly, they bought the house the very next day to block her from moving in. But Clara never got mad. She just laughed and thought it was funny that people were so ignorant.

From being in her class and hearing stories like this, I learned that Clara Luper was a fighter. I realized that if you believed in something, especially as it pertains to human rights, you don't back off. I learned not to judge people. Don't just "go with the flow." You have to stand up for your principles and what's right at any cost. If you get arrested, you get arrested. So far I haven't been, but Clara Luper taught me it's not wrong to get arrested for doing the right thing.

MR. HOMER HYDE

Homer Hyde also had a tremendous influence on my business and me personally. Homer Hyde founded Hyde Drug in 1939, a chain of pharmacies in Oklahoma City. I worked stocking shelves at Hyde Drug when I graduated from high school at only eighteen years old. I eventually worked my way up to manager.

Mr. Homer Hyde was an amazing business owner and man. To fully comprehend what I learned from Mr. Hyde, you have to understand the story of Hyde Drug. The shopping cart was invented in Oklahoma in 1937 for grocery stores. However, it was Homer Hyde who introduced the shopping cart into his pharmacies in the 1950s. It was the first drug store to do this, and the story made the news. This was the precursor to what pharmacies like Walgreens and CVS Pharmacy would later become.

Hyde Drug eventually expanded to nine stores, and it was amazing to me how Homer Hyde had so much control over the market in Oklahoma City. He controlled the market not just for ten years, but for almost fifty years! Walgreens would not even attempt to come into the Oklahoma City market until he closed down business. Another pharmacy, Eckerd Drugs, came into the market. They were continually opening and shutting down stores because they couldn't compete with Hyde Drug. Eckerd Drugs, and then Hyde Drug, was eventually bought out by CVS Pharmacy.

Mr. Homer Hyde taught me the value of customer service and customer loyalty. We would have customers buy a product from another store, maybe Eckerd Drugs. They would bring the product into our store to return. They wouldn't have a receipt but would claim it was purchased from a Hyde Drug store. We could look at the label and clearly see that wasn't the case. Mr. Hyde's philosophy was … it didn't matter; go ahead and take it back anyway. That's how he held such a tight hold on the market, by creating an atmosphere of outstanding customer service and fostering tremendous customer loyalty. I learned from Homer Hyde that if you do the right thing for the customer, you'll always win in the end.

MR. DAVID GREEN

The final person that had an incredible influence on me was David Green, the last employer I worked for before I started Kevo Properties in 2011. David Green is the founder of Hobby Lobby. There were about eighty-eight Hobby Lobby stores when I started working there. I worked in a 500,000-square-foot warehouse doing inventory control. I was in my late thirties when I started, and I worked with David for almost fourteen years while building my real estate career on the side.

In case you aren't familiar, Hobby Lobby is a craft store. When I started with them, they had about fourteen competitors. By the time I resigned in 2010, I was over operations and manufacturing, which meant I had about five hundred employees in my building. In the fourteen years I worked for David, the warehouse grew from 500,000 square feet to five million square feet. Now in just another ten years, they have close to ten million square feet.

The biggest influence David Green had on the company I run today was in processes and systems. At Hobby Lobby, we were the only distribution center that had to have special forklifts made because we put so many miles on them. All the products that get pushed out to the Hobby Lobby stores, and today there are around six hundred, come from one central warehouse. This is unheard of in today's market because even a Walmart will only ship to around thirty stores per warehouse. So, even though the industry had been doing it the same way for years, David believed there was another way to do it.

Another example of David's effective systems is how Hobby Lobby orders its products. David believed that you needed to depend on humans more than computers when ordering products. He always had a human place the orders because computers wouldn't know why you ran out of certain products. A computer isn't going to know the reason you ran out of red and white bandanas in Norman, Oklahoma, was because it was the University of Oklahoma Sooner Day. A computer also won't anticipate when that event is going to happen, but a human will. Because of that, David held the tightest inventory controls ever, and that lesson still sticks with me.

As I've named these life-changers for me, I'm sure it has you thinking about the men and women in your life who helped to form who and where you are today. From all of the bits and pieces I gathered from these four individuals, I ultimately learned you need to do things in your own way and in a right way.

You always need to keep your clients first, which in my case has always been REALTORS®. They're my clients. And in the end, if I keep doing what's best for them, my business will take care of itself.

Action: Take time to consider and write down how you have been influenced to this day. Recognizing who has impacted you enough to develop your belief system.

CHAPTER 10

Meeting Influencers

"A pessimist sees the difficulty in every opportunity; an optimist sees the opportunity in every difficulty."

-Winston Churchill

By now you understand this about me: I believe a person can't sit and wait for things to change in life. If I waited for the real estate industry to change before I launched out on my own, I would still be working at Hobby Lobby. Creating change means you're going to have to take risks. I'm not talking about risking your family or being unethical or immoral. I'm talking about "out-of-your-comfort-zone" types of risk that creates an opening for you to make a change. Calculated risks are best, where you can collect the most information and data, glean wisdom from others, and so on. For the most part, that's a great way to take a risk. At other times, you have to be like Peter in the Bible in Matthew 14, when Jesus was walking on the water and Peter said, "Lord, if it's You, tell me to come," and Jesus said, "Yes, come." Well, 'ol Peter took the risk without asking the others in the boat if it was a good idea. He didn't sit and calculate the options. He stepped out of the boat! Sometimes that's what you have to do in life to advance your career, especially when it's all dependent on you. … Take the step of faith and get out of the boat!

At one point in my career, I had to deal with a legal battle involving an online company. I began to see the need for help from our state government and I found out there was a position open for a real estate commissioner in Oklahoma, so I decided that I wanted the position!

This was an appointed position by the governor. Each year, the governor makes about three hundred to four hundred appointments, so it's a big shuffle and a lot of politics. To get an appointment, your state representative has to put in a word for you, but the governor has the final decision. Mary Fallin was governor of Oklahoma at the time. I had never met Governor Fallin. I think the only time I ever saw her was when she was eating in a restaurant in downtown Oklahoma City. I walked by and somebody said, "There's Mary Fallin."

I quickly realized that I couldn't rely on only one person to suggest my name to Mary Fallin. I would need multiple people to call her and say, "Hey, we need you to recommend Steve Burris to be the next real estate commissioner." I started calling and asking friends and acquaintances if they might know someone who knew Governor Fallin. Oftentimes, the person I spoke with gave me the phone number of people they knew. I would then cold call them and introduce myself (there's that "stepping out of the boat" idea!). I was given Larry Parman's phone number, who used to be the secretary of commerce for Oklahoma and knew Governor Fallin very well. After speaking with him, he called the governor to tell her what a wonderful candidate I would be.

I was networking like crazy, and my wife was trying to help as well. My wife knew Susan Coles, and we decided to call her. Susan Coles is the owner of Coles Garden, a wedding and event center in Oklahoma City. Not only that, Susan was good buddies with Governor Fallin. She took trips with her and actually stayed with the governor whenever she came into town. After our conversation, Susan also called the governor and recommended me for the appointment. After all the networking and calls, I eventually received the appointment.

To be successful, you have to be willing to get out there and network. Just talk to people. All these people I needed in my corner had a lot more influence than I had. It doesn't help much to try to find people that have the same or less influence than you. You have to be willing to go out there and meet people you know have much more influence. Influential people are mostly influential for a reason. They're nice people. In most cases, they're GREAT people that want to help and don't mind helping.

The idea of networking your way into success proved itself time and time again. In the past, if I wanted to raise money for a project, the first thing I did was go online. I would spend hours on YouTube. I would try to figure out how to make a pitch deck for investors, how much interest or percentage of the company they should get, and even how to value a company. I would literally spend hours researching all of this. I ended up with about ten books on the subject. I think I read half of one of them. Then I started realizing that it's much easier to network your way in that direction than trying to read about it and study it on your own.

For instance, at one point I was considering a project and the amount of money I would need to raise for this was between $20 million and $40 million. I was trying to think how in the world was I going to raise that much money? That's when I started networking. I called one of our brokers that works in the company, and he went to college with a guy named Daniel that makes investments and was the chief revenue officer (CRO) and chief financial officer (CFO) for Pegasus.

Pegasus was one of the first companies before Expedia and Travelocity. In the "olden days," a person had to book hotels individually. You'd have to call 1-800 numbers to contact different hotels and compare prices. Pegasus was the first software platform that connected all the hotels, and Daniel was part of that. Later, Expedia and Travelocity took that and became the next platform. Daniel was also a part of Zappos.com, the shoe company, and helped merge that into Amazon. He ended up working for Amazon for several years and has been a part of numerous other ventures.

Knowing that I needed to get connected to a really big player, I called my friend and he got a meeting set up with Daniel. In the meeting, I went through my presentation and he liked it. One of the parts had an Uber element in it, and Daniel said, "Hey, I know the guy that helped start Uber." That was amazing to me! I was meeting with the guy who was the CFO of a fund that does billion-dollar deals, probably one of the most prominent venture capitalist funds in the United States. And my friend, Daniel, was buddies with him and could get a meeting with him anytime he wanted to.

Daniel agreed to work with me to put the right presentation together. I could have spent hours and hours trying to figure all this out on my own, or I could call people that actually know what they're doing and know how to get right to the top. It is much easier to network than to go figure it all out on your own.

Most people don't like to walk into an unfamiliar situation such as opportunities like the many business events and luncheons that are available to attend regularly. If you're at all like me, going by yourself does not sound fun whatsoever. Here's an easy solution: If you know someone who is an extrovert and likes to talk all the time, hang out with them when you go to events. All you have to do is go to the event, and let the other person work the room with you. They're constantly saying things like, "Hey, this is Jim. Meet Steve. He's one of the best real estate agents in the country." The extrovert does all your introductions throughout the whole meeting because that's what they like to do. This makes it a lot more comfortable and easier to network. When you start going to these events, they kind of snowball. You will see some of the same people and you'll get invited to more. Charities and nonprofits regularly host some sort of event and they want as many people as possible to attend. When you get invited, plan to go and meet two to three new people. It will be another connection for your future.

After a while, you could probably be at a networking event every week. And here's the other great thing: When you get involved in a variety of groups, they start sending you emails. Guess what they include? Emails and names of hundreds of other people that are in the group. That makes it easy to get in front of a ton of people.

It's important to remember that you also need to meet the right people with influence. Let's say there's a big company in town that does a lot of relocations. You may want to get in with one of the executive secretaries or the human resources department. Both of these possibly influence the new people that are moving in their company and they can refer them to you. It might even be more effective to get to know the owner of the company, who can then tell everybody to use you. See how simple that becomes? You may be thinking, "That's crazy and scary!" But if you network this way and hit it off with them, you will build a relationship and become friends. When you have the CEO of the company say, "Hey, use Steve. He's the best agent in the country," that's the payoff for all of your work. You can't get that from a list of names you buy.

When you're networking with people that own companies, opportunities naturally arise. I began contemplating opening my own title company that would sell title insurance and do abstracting because I knew there was a lot of money in that. I started setting up appointments, networking with people that were in the business, and trying to find a way that I could start my own company.

One of the owners of the largest abstracting and title businesses in the state called me and set up a meeting. He offered to work with me and help me set up a company. He had all the experience and did all of the legal work. It was one of the most profitable ventures I've ever done, all from just knowing him. We have joined together for multiple other deals. When you are friends with people that happen to own big companies, doors open that would take you forever to open, or possibly even would never open otherwise.

These examples of my own story show how impactful and how powerful it is to network and meet people of influence. A lot of you are thinking, "That's not me, I'm a total introvert and the thought of walking onto a stage or walking into a network marketing meeting is overwhelming. I might as well be naked standing in the middle of the street!" Yet, I'm a total introvert (which is kind of funny that I'm in real estate since it means you meet people all the time) and have found a way to network successfully. Let me teach you.

My wife and I noticed something not too long ago about our daughter. We have one of the most outgoing, smiley, happy daughters on the planet. Elizabeth is a couple of years older than her brother, who plays football. The school was looking for volunteers to help with the football team. Since this would go toward the ninety hours of volunteer work she has to do before graduating, she signed up to help.

My wife and I noticed when she volunteered for the first time, she was really guarded. It was as if her "Miss Congeniality" button had been turned off. Before her second time, she asked if her friend, Addie, could go with her. We said, "Yes!" This time it was like her switch had been flipped back "on." The power of just having Addie by her side, who's an extreme introvert, gave Elizabeth the freedom to be her extroverted self. She was bouncing all over the place, it looked like she knew everybody everywhere, and it was the most exciting thing she'd ever done.

That's when it occurred to us that Elizbeth always travels with a buddy. She is the extrovert when she buddies up. Her buddy gives her the power and freedom to be who she is. That principle works, and it's nothing to be ashamed of at all!

Remember this when you're first starting in real estate: "Buddy up" with somebody. Buddy up to go to open houses together. Buddy up to go to For Sale by Owners. Buddy up when you go to networking meetings. Just buddy up. It doesn't matter if either one of you are big extroverts. Don't worry about that part of it. The power of not being alone gives you the strength to move through the experience much faster and more comfortably. I would start here. Use the buddy up system to get yourself out there and start connecting to people.

Action: Don't be afraid to ask successful people for help. Reach out to someone successful today. Find and go to networking events.

CHAPTER 11

Mindset & Motivation

"Never let people who chose the path of least resistance steer you away from your chosen path of most resistance."

- David Goggins

Zig Ziglar said, "People often say, motivation doesn't last. Well, neither does bathing, that's why we recommend it daily!" Motivation is important, but I'm concerned about the misconception that you have to be motivated all the time to be successful in this business. Motivation can come from the basic fact that you need to put food on your table and pay your bills. I'm not always 100 percent motivated when I wake up. It would be a little weird if that were the case. Some days I may only be 50 percent motivated, sometimes less. In any successful business, it takes you five years to get really good at it and ten years to become wealthy at it. That's obviously a long time. It's not possible for you to stay motivated 100 percent of that time. Remember all those "overnight successes" usually happened after ten thousand hours of investment into their art, sport, skill, etc.

Over the years, I've learned what keeps me from becoming sad or depressed. It's difficult to effectively work when someone feels that way. Since you have to work at least one to two hours every day growing and making your business better, I want to share with you what helps me. I have identified several personal keys to prevent me from slowing down and feeling yucky and help me feel motivated and optimistic. What works for you will be different, and you'll have to figure those out. The critical component is putting them into practice. Let's say I go to my hose connected to the faucet in my backyard, and I stand there waiting for the water to come out. I start getting frustrated and irritated because nothing is happening. In fact, I'm about to throw the hose down and quit! My wife comes out and asks me what I'm doing. To which I'm going to respond with a snippy comment like, "Isn't it obvious? I'm watering the plants! Duh!" To which she's going to ask me how that's going to happen without turning on the faucet! I could say what I want to happen, plan what I want to happen, wish for it, pray for it, but if I don't do what makes the water come out, those plants aren't going to get watered. The same is true for our lives. If we don't do the things that help us to stay on track, we can wish and pray for success, but without working the keys, we will stand there without anything happening, or worse, we'll quit!

Use what you want from the keys to my success, then create

your own, and put them into practice.

KEY ONE: Rest

When you don't get enough rest, it affects how you feel the entire day. I go to bed around 1:00 a.m. and I'm up by 7:00 a.m., sometimes even by 6:00 a.m., but for my body this is enough sleep. I seem to operate better that way. I feel groggy if I sleep too long. I stay up until 1:00 a.m. or 2:00 a.m. at times sitting outside, looking at the stars, and just being. This is when I do some of my best thinking, when I'm alone with my thoughts. No television, no phone calls, nobody talking to me, no distractions. It's amazing what your brain can do when there are no distractions. Additionally, I feel grateful when I'm outside looking up, noticing how big the universe is.

KEY TWO: The Three E's–Eating Right, Exercise, and Excuses.

Let's start with the first "E": <u>eating right</u>. I have trouble controlling what I put in my mouth. If I start out eating a salad with taco meat in it, then I want chips and salsa to go with it. You need to figure out when you're most productive and make your eating habits fit that. I barely eat anything in the mornings because I'm most productive from 7:00 a.m. to 1:00 p.m. After that point, I start going downhill and it's usually after I've eaten. If I'm trying to stay motivated and get more done, I sometimes won't eat at all. I'll skip my meals all day until I get home around 4:00 p.m. to 6:00 p.m. I actually feel more energetic when I intermittently fast. I'm not saying I'm a doctor or that this is how you should eat. I'm probably wrong, but I'm telling you what works for me, what motivates me, and what keeps my energy level moving. You have to find out what works for you. And the added benefit of this is you will drop some weight if you don't eat all day. That's how it works.

Now let's move on to the second "E": <u>exercise</u>. I would love to tell you I exercise every day, but I'm not one of those people that's disciplined enough to go to the gym every day. I'll do it for a while, then I'll quit. But I have found ways to trick myself into exercising.

I used to hear that it's stupid to mow your own yard (especially since I have almost half an acre). If I was going to take that same amount of time to be productive and make money, I would agree. But honestly, I'm not.

So, I switched my exercising at a gym to taking care of my yard. I mow it, edge it, and weed eat it. It takes me almost two hours, and I'm walking the entire time. I use a push mower since a riding mower would defeat my purpose. I end up walking almost two miles back and forth around my yard, and I usually mow my yard three times a week. For me, I feel better when I sweat, and this is one way I trick myself into exercising.

The final "E" is <u>excuses</u>. One of the things that is very demotivating is constant worry about the lack of control in your life. You truly have very little control. You have family issues that come up, arguments with your spouse, problems with your kids, and people sometimes say untrue words about you and may even sue you. You can't control these things. If you put your energy on all negative things, I guarantee it's not going to move your business forward.

Many of our problems stem from trying to be in control or controlling those around us. We think if our kids would just listen to us, they could avoid the pain we went through. Sometimes yes, but trying to avoid pain in one area usually just ends up with us having to face it somewhere else. When we are always trying to "fix" a problem, it can really be a form of control. Although we can control some things, like what we're going to eat or other simple things, we can't control what the economy will do. We can't control what other people are going to do, no matter how much we love them. We can control our response to them. We are in 100 percent control of our responses. We may be a work-in-progress in this area, but awareness is the first step to change, so no more excuses!

KEY THREE: Capture Your Thoughts

One of the most difficult things people struggle with, including me, is letting go of the things that you cannot control. All that time you spend worrying takes away time in your day to be productive. And 99 percent of what you worry about never even happens anyway. Seriously, 99 percent.

But how do you control this? The Bible says to take every thought captive. When I read that, I thought, "You've got to be kidding. I can't control any of my thoughts and I am never going to get to the point where I'm controlling them."

One of the biggest struggles I've had was about four years ago. My oldest son passed away at twenty-five from complications related to him being a heroin addict. I quickly realized that I had to pass by the hospital he died in every day on my way to and from work. Every time I got close to the hospital, I would cycle through about fifteen minutes of horrible thoughts about my son and how he died. After a while, I recognized I was allowing my thoughts to take control and wander into this depressive line of thinking.

It seems natural. If we always associate something with a bad experience how in the world can we change it? You can't change your memories. There are going to be things that trigger them, like the hospital did for me. What I learned I could do was replace the negative memories with positive ones. There were eighteen years of my son's life that were awesome. He was my first-born son, and for those first eighteen years he was a great guy. This is what I call my "replacement system." As soon as I started having negative thoughts about my son, I replaced them with positive ones instead. I immediately think about the other eighteen years of his life and the good memories I had and drew upon those images. To this day, when I drive by the hospital, I still have to intentionally do this. Starting out it would take me about five minutes to replace the negative thoughts with good ones. Then it got down to two minutes, then one minute. Now it's only about five seconds before I actually feel good when I'm going by the hospital. So far, this technique is the only way I've been able to capture my negative thoughts.

79

Everybody has negative people in their life. There are probably few horrible people on the whole planet, but all of us seem to meet at least one of them at some point. Whenever these negative people come into your life, begin the process of thinking about what benefit you received from them.

Maybe someone embezzled and stole money from you. The benefit you received is that you've learned your lesson, and you are now more vigilant with your finances. Perhaps a friend or acquaintance said something horrible about you. Your radar went off in the beginning with this person. You knew they had talked about other people in the past and that you probably shouldn't hang out with them. But you still chose to be around this person. Maybe the benefit you received is to trust your instincts. Instead of blaming them, think about what you could have done better, what you could have done to avoid the negative situation. You will start to have a positive attitude, and the negative situation will become a positive.

Switching your thoughts around may feel instinctively backwards, but if you stay with it, you'll find yourself switching faster and faster. Then it will become more automatic for other situations.

KEY FOUR: Dream Boards

I've heard about dream boards my whole life and I thought they were a joke. They seemed silly, like something for a teenager. But now, my wife and I have a dream board together. My children both have dream boards in their bedrooms. I wish I would have started one at an earlier age.

My first dream board was twenty years ago. I put everything up on that dream board that I could imagine I wanted—how many agents, cars, trips, houses, anything I could think of at that point. Well, in fifteen years, everything on that board was completed, all checked off, all done. I still have my old dream board. It looks like a mess, but a fifteen-year-old dream board gets messy. My wife created a new dream board for us with all new things on it. What goes on your dream board is just whatever you can imagine. What I envision today is a lot bigger than what I could have envisioned twenty years ago.

I know that writing down your goals and reading them out loud every day is something you're supposed to do. I'm going to be honest. I have written down my goals in the past, but I've never read them daily like you are supposed to do. I'm not saying writing all your goals down is wrong because there's too much history that says it's right. That system just doesn't work for me.

The dream board is more successful for me because I can look at it. I put it in places where I have to walk past it. I put it right inside the door from the garage to the house so that I have to walk past it every time I leave the house or come back. The visual aid of the dream board motivates me. Essentially, everything on my dream board is my goal.

KEY FIVE: Motivational Tools

Another way to stay motivated is watching videos. You have to figure out who speaks to you. Jim Rome is a big inspiration to me, so I've watched and listened to him for years. I hang out with a lot of twenty-five-year-old's, and most of them think he's a horrible speaker and can't stand to listen to him. They'd rather listen to Tony Robbins, who I can't stand. He's just too loud for me.

Everyone is different and you have to figure out who inspires you. And here's the other thing: You have to accept what they're saying. That's part of our problem. To keep yourself motivated you can't go through the motion of just listening to what they're saying.

All motivational speakers say almost the same thing in their own voice and in their own stories. The problem is for years and years I heard what they were saying, but I didn't accept it. When you start to accept it as truth, then it will start motivating you long term. Motivationally, if you accept what they're saying is the truth and you operate in that truth, it will change the way you think, and you'll see your life change immediately.

KEY SIX: Just Show Up

Ninety percent of being successful is just showing up and working all the time. You have a 90 percent chance of success at what you're doing if you will just show up and do the work. The problem is 90 percent of everybody quits. When I thought about quitting, I always enjoyed the fact that I knew everybody else was quitting. I don't know what that says about my ego, but I enjoyed the fact that I had the option. I could quit if I wanted to, but it was my active decision not to quit.

Even if things were bad, I enjoyed it more knowing almost everybody else would quit. Something bad would happen, maybe running out of money. Well, that's a good reason to quit. Any one reason is enough to quit. Yet, when you realize everybody else quits with any of those reasons, you can enjoy it and feel good that you're overcoming it by just showing up.

Now, the last 10 percent of winning is just a dogfight. The difference between people making half a million and a million, that's in the top 10 percent. It's a dogfight and whoever wants to fight the hardest to get there succeeds.

KEY SEVEN: Follow Up

One of the biggest things people don't know how to do correctly is follow up. This drives me crazy! Follow up is something I harp on with my agents and is one of the keys to working in real estate. Whether you're calling a For Sale by Owner, a new prospective buyer, or a new prospective listing, you have to follow up every single week, sometimes for months and months. That's the way the business works. You have to learn how to follow up and what to say when you're following up. It's so important I'll say it three times: follow up, follow up, follow up! If you do, your business will work.

I'll give you an analogy. There are hundreds of books on how to lose weight. It seems like a new one comes out almost every week. There are books that tell you to only eat peanuts, only eat meat, only eat green foods, or only eat yellow foods on Mondays. There seems to be endless diets out there, and each one tells you something different. Dieting is simple. If you want to lose weight: eat less, move more. Very simple concept.

It's simple in real estate, too. If you want to be successful: meet people, follow up. I'll say it again, so you don't miss it. Meet people, follow up. If you'll at least do that, you're going to have the beginnings of a successful career.

Now, between when you're meeting people and following up, work on all of the rest of your skill sets. Just like with eating less and moving more, you can work on eating healthier foods. You can work on your exercise routine to make it better.

At its most basic, real estate comes down to two things. Meet people, follow up! Do this, and you'll make it.

Action: Find what motivates you. If you don't know, then start with one of my "keys."

CHAPTER 12

Books That Inspire

"Sleep is for people without access to the MLS."

-Lighter Side of Real Estate

There have been a few books in my life that have inspired me and had great influence on my life. It's actually rare if I read an entire book. I have a heap of books on my shelf, but I haven't "read" most of them. Generally, everything I do is audible. I've worn out tons of CDs in my car listening to books. Since everything is online, that's how I listen. I'm going to go through some of the books that inspired me and tell you what I got out of them. They're not in any order of importance because they all had true power and influence in my life.

Think and Grow Rich by Napoleon Hill

What I found interesting in this book is that successful people, like the Carnegies and Henry Ford, had a pattern for what made them successful. If you know that there's a pattern, then all you have to do is follow their pattern. It's much easier to follow a path that somebody has already cut.

I mostly listened to it online. It's an extremely long book, maybe two inches thick, but it has good information and is worth reading. The other thing you should also do is read about the author, Napoleon Hill. He was a character, and his history is very interesting (note how many years it took him to write the book).

How to Master the Art of Selling by Tom Hopkins

Tom Hopkins was one of the few REALTORS® in the United States that has ever sold 365 houses in one year. That's right, a house a day. The version that I read was probably from the late eighties to the early nineties, so some of the things he talked about in the book were a little outdated.

I do need to give you a heads up before reading this book, though: It's difficult to follow how Tom Hopkins' sales career went. In my opinion, it's too complicated. Even so, it will be more beneficial for you than any other book because it's written specifically for real estate.

You can flip to a chapter and he teaches you the basics of selling, such as alternative choice and porcupine questions. He's also really good at teaching you how to paint pictures with words, saying the right words to the right person at the right time, and showing how this will make all the difference in the world. One thing I love about this book is that it's very straight to the point. If you need to know more about open houses, you can go straight to the chapter on that without having to even read the entire book. It's basically a training book for real estate, and I've used it for years.

Turning the Flywheel by Jim Collins

This book didn't have as much impact on me in becoming an agent, but it did have an influence on how I built my company. The "flywheel" concept is that all great companies have a pattern, along with individual salespeople.

Companies like Amazon have a flywheel and every action that is taken forces the company to another action, which leads to another action, which ends up right back where it started. For instance, Amazon offers tons of products, which gets people to go online to order them. They deliver extremely fast. The experience is good, and then the customers come back to buy more products. That's their flywheel.

Jim Collins also wrote the book Good to Great, another worthwhile book, but Turning the Flywheel was the most impactful book I have read on how a company becomes successful and why. Everybody should understand how their own business runs; create a visual of your company's flywheel to illustrate how it operates. When you're communicating to another company, show them the visual so everybody can look at it together and be on the same page.

Traction: Get a Grip on Your Business by Gino Wickman

This is a great book for understanding how to build strategic plans. Again, this is more of a company book, but it's also good for an individual REALTOR® because it teaches you how to start taking action items quickly. I've done strategic planning where you ask yourself, what are we going to be doing in ten years? What are all the steps we need to take to get there? About 80 percent of the companies that do strategic planning almost never follow through with those plans because it usually comes down to execution.

Traction shows you how to set up and create action plans immediately and get people to start moving in that direction. That way, you have traction. Wickman makes it easy to understand how to get a game plan, how to hold yourself accountable, and how to hold others accountable. This is a great book that had a huge influence on me.

Rocket Fuel: The One Essential Combination That Will Get You More of What You Want from Your Business by Gino Wickman and Mark C. Winters

This is an interesting book and it helped me define what role I played in the company. I think it's an excellent book for anybody to read if you want to know if you're a visionary or an integrator. What role do you play?

When you start to understand who you are, you'll understand who you need to pull around you. This book has personality type tests. By taking these tests, you will know exactly who you are, and it will show you your strengths. Just as important, if not more so, it will show you your weaknesses. If you understand what your weaknesses are, you can work on them or stay away from them.

You have to continue to work on yourself. Real estate is essentially a self-improvement plan in progress. Working on yourself results in more money. The longer you work on yourself and the more discipline you have to make yourself better, your income rises proportionately.

The Millionaire Real Estate Agent by Gary Keller

Gary Keller's book inspired me as I built our company. He talks about how to build teams. The concept of buyer agents and selling agents helped me understand that teams are the best way to go. If you're thinking about getting into the real estate business or even quitting the business, I encourage you to join a team because that's the best place for you to learn.

Less than 10 percent of agents in the United States are on a team. According to Gary Keller, teams are by far the best way to make the most amount of money. That's where you will learn the most and will have the highest success rate. You have almost an 80 percent chance to succeed if you join a team. In contrast, you have less than a 10 percent chance of making it if you're not on a team. There are approximately 1.4 million agents. You do the math.

The Science of Getting Rich by Wallace Wattles

The first time I listened to this book, me being from Oklahoma, I thought, my gosh, this is all new age stuff. I almost didn't hear half of it the first time. Being raised Southern Baptist, just the thought of saying "getting rich" was new to me; I thought all rich people were going to hell. I have a friend who jokes, "If that's the case, just tell me how much money you need to be rich. If it's $1 million a year, then I'm going to make $999,000! I'll stand on that threshold." But good news, God wants to bless us.

The author of this book, Wallace Wattles, was a Christian writer. The funny thing is, he wrote it in 1890 and was talking about the Carnegies. It breaks down how the universe or God works in your favor if you're doing the right things. It's an odd book to read or listen to because it talks about this thinking stuff, and here's what I concluded from this: thoughts are things. Whatever you think about happens, and the Bible confirms this. Not 100 percent, of course, but what you dwell on, what you think about, is what you manifest.

Nothing in the universe was created without thought first. For example, every time you drive down the street in your neighborhood, you stop at a stop sign. There was thought before that stop sign was created. The metal pole and the concrete that holds it, somebody thought about that. Somebody thought about the bolts that hold it together. There was an engineer. Somebody designed it. Somebody decided how big it should be, how tall, the color, the font. There was an enormous amount of thought by multiple people to create a stop sign. How many stop signs should there be? Which side of the street? How close to the intersection? How far away from the curb? It goes on and on. Thought is where everything starts.

One of the biggest things I learned from The Science of Getting Rich is that you should stop and think. That's the whole premise of the book. Think first, and then grow and be rich. God gave you a brain and wants you to use it. You can't move through life going from task to task, reacting to everything. Think about it. Think about what you want to happen and what you're going to do. Think about where your life is going. As you start thinking about these things, it will lead to other thoughts about how to achieve what you want. Then, act on those thoughts.

The Bible

The Bible is one of the books I definitely recommend reading. One thing I learned from the Bible and how it relates to business is that it shows you who people are. The Bible has example after example of people who have failed and why. This is all good to understand because you're going to work around a lot of people. The Bible also has an infinite amount of knowledge and great one-liners. When things get tough, one of the things I've always used as a company is the wheat and the tares (or weeds) analogy (Matthew 13:24-30).

After you've planted your wheat crop, when things begin to grow, the wheat and the weeds grow about the same pace. Sometimes it's hard to distinguish one from the other. How-

90

ever, as the wheat continues to grow, the top of it becomes so heavy from the weight of the grain that it starts to bow down. The weeds don't bow. The weeds stand up and you can easily see them.

When you have an organization as large as ours, you sometimes have some bad actors, and everybody tends to want to rip them out. The point is to let God handle the weeds, because when the harvest comes in, that's when they are separated from the wheat. It's been my experience that the people I've been around that were weeds always work themselves out. If you are there and doing the right thing, the bad actors can't take it forever. They will leave on their own.

The Bible is a great reference place to get a ton of great stories and knowledge. Many of the stories will make you feel better about yourself when things are rough. I know when I'm going through tough times, I think about Christ dying on the cross. Then I ask myself, is what I'm going through really that tough? Is the price I'm paying that big? This gives me strength when I feel like quitting.

Real Estate Mentoring by Steve Burris

Of course I'll include mine! My book exists for the purpose of reminding you that you can thrive, no matter what "curve-ball" life might throw at you.

Side note: Why did we use "curve-ball" for analogies when it comes to life? A curve-ball is a baseball pitch that is used to keep the hitters off-balance. Wow! Conversely, I hope that reading my book will prove to you that in spite of those parts of life that can make you feel "off-balance," you can persevere and win!

Action: Decide if you are an audio reader or paper reader. Download or buy one of my suggested reads today. Read it three times before moving on. Many race to finish a book, so they miss the finer points. If the books aren't changing you, you aren't reading them enough.

CHAPTER 13

Keeping Real Estate Simple

"Real estate is an imperishable asset, ever increasing in value. It is the most solid security that human ingenuity has devised. It is the basis of all security and about the only indestructible security."

-Russell Sage

This chapter is very short because it wouldn't make any sense to say, "Keep real estate simple," and go on for twenty-five pages. Whenever one of my agents comes into the office complaining about being tired, I always ask them, "Are you really working?" Let's get down to the real work of real estate.

First, we need to define real work. Real work is negotiating a contract, calling on a listing to try to get it, trying to recruit a new person for your team, contacting a past client, prospecting, or trying to find new business. These are real things, real activities, real work. Once you've found a buyer and have the house under contract, the rest of it is just the administrative part, setting up inspections, paperwork, that sort of thing. This does not create new income; it's just completing the transaction. Therefore, it's not real work. Real work is activities that create income.

I used to have my agents wear a stopwatch. They would start the timer whenever they did any of these activities to see how long they really worked in a day. The longest I ever had anyone spend on those activities in an entire day was forty-two minutes. Keep in mind these were all $100,000+ earners. Time yourself if you have to, but you have to be very clear what real work is.

I developed an easy-to-remember system a long time ago that defines what you need to know about working in real estate. It's nothing original, it's just very specific and something I teach all of my agents. It is F.O.N.T. This stands for: For Sale by Owners, Open houses, Networking, and Teambuilding. If you notice and think about it, For Sale by Owners is dealing directly with people. Having open houses is dealing directly with people. Networking is dealing directly with people. And team building is definitely dealing directly with people.

I believe doing these things is the only real way this business works. A lot of agents try a lot of different things to get new business, but they're all a load of crap. Sending out postcards, load of crap. Billboards, load of crap. Making videos, you guessed it, load of crap. These things may all seem glamorous. Don't kid yourself. None of these things will give you long-term success. Some agents spend more time thinking about their business cards than they do actually thinking about how they're going to work an open house. That is ridiculous! There are no substitutes for F.O.N.T.

In conjunction with F.O.N.T., you have to become an expert at talking to people. You've got to know people, and you've got to become likable. Remember, the house isn't the product, you are. That's why I drive all my agents to meet people directly.

Also important is managing your schedule. In Tom Hopkins's book, How to Master the Art of Selling, one of the things he talks about is alternative choice. You can't schedule all over the place or stop what you're doing at the drop of a hat to meet with someone. You're never going to get anything done correctly if you do that.

Instead, you should employ the alternative choice method. Let's say you call a For Sale by Owner and ask if you can come see their house. If they agree to let you, you can't simply ask, "When do you want me to come over?" That's like asking ten people where they want to go eat dinner. Can you imagine all of the back and forth and the likelihood of everyone agreeing on one place? That almost never works.

You need to ask alternative questions instead.
The conversation would go like this:

"I've got Tuesday and Thursday open this week.
Which is better for you?"

They pick Thursday.

"Great. Do you like mornings, afternoons, or evenings?"

They prefer evenings.

"Super. I've got from 4:00-5:00 p.m. or 6:00-7:00 p.m.
Which time works for you?"

They choose from 6:00-7:00 p.m.

You just controlled the conversation. You managed how you got the appointment at the time you wanted to have it. That's what I mean by using alternative choices and controlling your schedule.

Action: Plan for three to five skills you want to increase in the next thirty days. Tackle one to two at a time.

CHAPTER 14

How to Get Rich

"There have been few things in my life which have had a more genial effect on my mind than the possession of a piece of land."

-Harriet Martineau

There are several ways to get rich. A lot of them weren't an option for me. One way is to become a professional athlete or an actor. I'm going to say that's probably not possible for 99 percent of us. If you could save $200 a month for forty years and had at least a 12 percent rate of return you can become a millionaire. Of course, forty years from now I don't know how much $1 million will buy, but that's one way to do it. You could save 25 to 30 percent of your income out of every single paycheck. That should probably do it. It would require a lot of discipline, but you could become rich that way.

None of these options seemed right for me. Luckily, there's another way. You can earn a profit from mastering something. Learn a skill, work on that skill for five to ten years, then teach that skill to other people. When I picked real estate, I invested the time, and I was teachable. I learned early that the bigger team you build in real estate, the more money you can make.

A parable from the Bible demonstrates this and makes sense, especially if you're a broker or a leader of a big team. This is how you have to think about people because it's true. I may butcher it, but here it goes.

In the Parable of the Sower (Luke 8), the farmer went out into his field and began throwing out seeds. Some of the seeds landed on rocks. Since seeds can't grow on rocks, they quickly ended up dying. Some of the seeds landed in bad soil—maybe it was too sandy, too wet, or too dry. The seeds couldn't flourish and died right away. Some of the seeds landed among the thorns and began to grow, but were choked out by the thorns. Some seeds were thrown out and immediately eaten by the crows. These seeds never had a chance to grow. And finally, there were some seeds that landed in fertile soil. These are the ones that thrived and produced the entire crop. Of all the seeds that the farmer threw out, only 25 percent of them prospered.

This parable is still relevant today and is the same with people. Only 25 percent of the people you try to work with will be successful. I know this to be true. We have a real estate school and only 25 percent of those that begin ever graduate. But just like the parable, these agents are the ones that will grow, thrive, and succeed.

When building your business with either clients or agents (and at this point in my career I only focus on recruiting agents), you should think of them as the seeds from the parable. Sometimes there's nothing you can say to a buyer or seller to get them to choose you. They landed on the rocks and you can't make them work with you. Some are like the seeds in the difficult soil. These are difficult people that you probably don't want to work with anyway.

Sometimes the crows get your clients. With me, the crows sometimes pluck agents out of my business and pull them into somebody else's business. When this happens, there's nothing you can do about it. Don't become negative or lose sight of what's happening because 75 percent of the opportunities you throw out there aren't going to produce a crop for you. Instead, focus on doing your best while working with the 25 percent.

Here's another analogy that I think will help. I love tomatoes. Every year I try to grow tomatoes and it's always a challenge. It's also fun to watch what happens with these tomato plants. Each year, I plant eight tomato plants pretty much in the same area. One of the plants will produce fifty tomatoes a day, while another plant is lucky to produce ten. Both plants are pretty much in the same location and the same soil. They basically get the same exact amount of water and nutrients. Yet one plant within two feet of the other plant produces ten times more.

At the beginning of the year when I put my tomato plants in the ground, I can't pick the plants that will produce the most; there's no way for me to know. I have to take care of all of them, treat them all equally. The plants that sometimes look the best are sometimes the ones who produce the least.

People are the same way. You can't predict the people who will produce the most. That's why when you look at people, or agents, you have to assume they're all going to produce a hundred times what they make. You have some REALTORS® that will come in and only sell six homes a year, some will sell thirty, and some will sell ninety. There's no way to tell which person will produce the most, so you have to take care of all of them.

Action: Think of two people that you could pull into your business to work with you. Even working as a group will bring success.

CHAPTER 15

Paying the Price

*"Whether you're an obstetrician or a third-grade
teacher or a real estate agent, you know when you're
doing good work. You're passionate about it."*

-Susan Isaacs

I think we all have heard in sports and business that you have to "pay the price." Honestly, I had no idea what that actually meant as far as my business. Does that mean you have to work one hundred hours a week? Does that mean that I should borrow a bunch of money or go broke? What exactly does "pay the price" mean? Through my own experiences, I want to break down what "pay the price" has felt like in my own life.

Bad stuff will happen to you along the way. Bad things will happen to your family. People will disappoint you, steal from you, and embezzle money from you. All these things are going to happen in some form. However, most of these things could have been avoided had you not picked the wrong people.

Therefore, in some way, you're going to have to pay the price for those choices. You have to own it and pay the price. Yes, someone took your last dollar. Yes, someone got you in a hole. Yes, someone sued you. It's still your fault, and you have to face the consequences of your choices. The key is that you have to keep pushing through if you're going to be successful.

Another way you will have to "pay the price" is with your time. You will have to work late at the office sometimes. You will work evenings and weekends. You will miss events that you wanted to attend. Sometimes these are professional events, but more times than not, it's personal.

You're going to make your family mad at times because you're still working at 10:00 p.m. You may not be physically at work, but you'll still be working. Mentally, you'll be trying to figure something out, trying to solve a problem. This is a price you will pay, and there's no way around it.

Sometimes the price you pay is financial. Over a ten-year time period, I started out with very little money. Around my eighth and ninth year, I was making ten to fifteen times more money, but still felt like I didn't have any. I was always reinvesting the money back into the company, back into myself.

You have to make sure that your business survives by reinvesting. Everyone may not understand, your family included, but that's what you have to do if you want to get to the next level. You could choose to back off, try to hover, and stay at the same level. But you should know that your business is either growing or it's dying. You don't get to just stand still. For your business to grow, you have to pay the price financially.

Paying the price is not fun. This is when you have to remember that you're doing something that is worthwhile and makes a difference. It doesn't matter the price you're paying because you're still moving forward. And don't forget, you're doing something that most people would have quit a long time ago.

You have to define what you think a win is. Maybe your goal was to sell three houses in a month. If you do that, that's a win. You have to set goals for yourself and know what a win is for you. Otherwise, you could sell ten houses in a month and still not feel like a winner because you didn't hit a goal. Define what your win is.

Even though the picture I painted of having to pay the price may sound sad or depressing, I would gladly pay that price a thousand times over. What you have to understand is that no matter what you do, you're going to pay some kind of price. Consider the price you'll pay if you don't do what I'm suggesting. Your price may be that your kids can't go to the school of your choosing and they can't receive the education you want for them. Your price may be that you can't pay for medical insurance for yourself and your family.

You might not be able to fix the refrigerator or the car when they break down, and you certainly can't afford to buy new ones. You may not be able to take care of your parents when they get older and can't live on their own. You may not be able to retire. Instead, you'll be living paycheck to paycheck for the next eighty years.

You have to choose the path you want to take. The reality is if you don't choose a path, one is chosen for you. And it's never the path where you end up with a bunch of money. It's never the path where you choose whether you want the green Lamborghini or the yellow one. It's never the path where you have to decide if you want to go to the Bahamas or ski in Switzerland for your next vacation. Those are the types of choices you get to make by choosing the right path and paying the price.

You will pay the price in one way or another. Either way, it's your choice. To me, there's only one real option. Choose to pay the price for ten years or however long it takes to make your company a success, and then pay the price as you go. In the end, you get to live the rest of your life pretty much how you would like to have it. In the end, paying the price is always worth it.

Action: Get out your calendar and write the times that you will work. Establish dedicated times for focused work.

CHAPTER 16

Get Out There

"In the real estate business you learn more about people, and you learn more about community issues, you learn more about life, you learn more about the impact of government, probably more than any other profession that I know of."

-Johnny Isakson

Some agents think you can be successful in the real estate business without meeting people face-to-face. But, I'm here to tell you that's not the case. You won't be successful by sending out postcards, putting up billboards, or any other type of marketing you can think of that doesn't involve face-to-face contact with a human.

I've had some people say they've tried different things and had success because they landed two buyers. I don't care if you get a couple of buyers every once in a while, that's not sustainable. The only way to have long-lasting success is to get out there face-to-face.

The reason we don't want to get out there is because we're all scared to death. Scared of what? Rejection. Think about it. As we grow up, we're told by our parents to be quiet and not bug people. We're told that we should be seen and not heard.

Consequently, we grow up with the same attitude. We stop talking because we think anything that we say is going to bug people, especially if we think we're going to make money from talking to them. We really feel weird then. That is so crazy. Get over it!

The only way you're going to get over the fear of rejection is by getting out there and doing what makes you feel uncomfortable. Is it awkward? You bet it is. Did it make me feel awkward calling on "For Sale by Owners" and people I didn't really know? Yes! The only way over that fear was to pick up the phone and make the call.

Did it make me feel weird calling on rich people I was associated with and asking them to help me get buyers, sellers, and new agents? It most definitely did. But you know what? That fear was going to keep me broke. You have to pick how you want to live. I made the decision that I would face my fear, I would deal with the awkwardness at times because I would rather be a millionaire.

You can't let your fear stop you from asking for help. Here's the thing. People really don't care that much about you. They're not sitting around thinking, "Steve called and asked for help getting a buyer so he must be broke." People don't think that way. You have to reprogram your thinking about this. Most people want to help you if you let them.

When I worked in retail, I found that rich people asked for the biggest discounts. It's not that they needed the discount, but rich people don't mind asking for help. That's what your mindset needs to be. If you don't want to ask for help, you're thinking like a poor person. If you are willing to ask for help, you're now thinking like a rich person. Decide who you want to be and start thinking that way and acting that way.

If you're doing something and it's uncomfortable, that's usually a sign that you're doing the right thing. Your brain has one function when you're born. Your brain's job is to protect you, to not let anything bad happen to you. It protects you from physical harm, but it also protects your feelings.

From a very young age, if you get too close to the edge of something that's really high, you're hit with fear. That's your brain protecting you and telling you to back up. If you reach up and touch something on the stove that's hot, without thinking, you immediately yank back your hand. Again, that's your brain operating to protect you.

Your brain does the same thing whenever something makes you feel uncomfortable. It wants to protect you and tells you to stop doing whatever it is that's making you uneasy.

If you are going to listen to your feelings and your emotions in any business, and especially in the real estate industry, you're going to end up financially broke. Your feelings don't matter. It's your actions that count. Move through your actions and your feelings will follow, and your life will change.

Action: Get comfortable with "no." Ask several people for something, even something small. Keep going until you have gotten at least five "nos."

CHAPTER 17

What's Wrong with Getting Rich?

*"Land monopoly is not only monopoly, but it is
by far the greatest of monopolies; it is a perpetual
monopoly, and it is the mother of all other forms of
monopoly."*

-Winston Churchill

Depending on your mindset, "rich" is a bad word. Growing up Southern Baptist, I think there was a dollar amount where we were possibly going to go to hell if you made over that amount. My goal, then, was to find out what that dollar amount was and make a little bit below that amount. I'm kidding, but people often look at being rich from the wrong perspective.

Can poor people help anybody? Poor people need help. Rich people are the only ones who can help others. You may say that you can volunteer. Well, does that mean you don't ever have to work? Could you maybe volunteer more if you had more money?

Being rich is not the most important thing. It's probably up there with air, though. If you think about it, money controls almost every decision you make every single day. Almost every hour, you have to make a decision based on money first.

If you say that you don't think about money and it's not important to you, try not thinking about it for a day. When you get up and go to a job that you may not like, is that because of money? Obviously, that means you do things because of money. You go to work somewhere you don't like because you don't have enough money to stay home.

When you pick a restaurant, do you pick it based on what it might cost? Does it even enter your head? Then when you go to the restaurant, do you ever look at the prices and decide what you'll order based on those prices?

When you send your kids to school, do you send them to private school or public school? If you believe they should go to public school because it's the best thing for them, that's great. If you're making your decision solely based on the fact that you can't afford to send them any other place, then there's the money issue again. What about college? Do you ever worry about how you're going to pay for your children's college?

How about your healthcare? Do you ever get sick to your stomach when you think about having to take your kid to the doctor? When you take your child to the doctor of course, it's because you want that doctor to help your child. But you're also thinking about the money, about how much it's going to cost at the doctor's office. You're not a bad parent, you're normal.

You need to get over the notion that being rich is somehow bad and that you shouldn't talk about it. Let's define rich. My definition of rich is buying anything I want, going anywhere I want to go, and doing what I want to do on my own terms.

Benjamin Franklin ran a newspaper. That was his profession and how he made money. He was also an inventor. That was his passion. Because he made enough money in the printing business, he got to follow his passion. He was able to let loose his creative ability because he had the freedom to pursue it. That's what money did for him.

You can be more creative to express yourself when money doesn't hinder you. That's what money does; it allows you to express yourself. It allows you to give. It allows you to change somebody else's life. It allows you to do things that are otherwise limited by money or the lack of it.

If you want to work in a foreign country, maybe in Africa, building water wells, wouldn't it be wonderful if you had the money to go do it? Wouldn't it be amazing to be able to express yourself by doing what you really want to do? That's what being rich can do for you.

Even the Bible talks about what you should do with your money in the Parable of the Talents in Matthew 25:14-30. In this story, a master gives money (called talents) to three of his servants. He tells them to invest the money and go do something with it. Two of the servants did just that and doubled their money. When they returned to the master to show him, he rewarded them by giving them more money. However, the third servant was too scared to do anything with his money. He was too afraid he would lose it, so he hid the money, and buried it in his backyard. When he returned to the master and told him what he had done, his master was extremely upset with him and took the money back. Think about what God (represented by the master) did here. He took the money back because the servant was too afraid to take a risk. You have to start rethinking what it means to be rich. You have to look at it differently. God is telling you that you need to do something with your money.

Action: Decide what being rich means to you. Write below the thing you are wanting most.

CHAPTER 18

When Is It Over?

"If you don't own a home, buy one. If you own a home, buy another one. If you own two homes, buy a third."

-John Paulson

When is it over? When will it end? That's the big question you may be asking. Do you ever get to stop working? Let's look at when you ask if you can stop working.

I'm here to tell you that if you're getting up every morning and going to a job that you think is work, you're in the wrong business. You should be doing something that you love to wake up and do every day. I'm not saying do it for free, but you should love what you do. I do; it doesn't feel like work to me. When you understand that you should be doing what God gave you the talent to do, and you go out and do that, it's no longer work. The minute you realize this is the minute you feel like you've retired.

Does that mean you sit on your couch all day watching TV? Does it mean that you lay on a beach all the time? Heck no! And why would you want to do that anyway? Don't get me wrong. I like the beach just as much as the next guy. I like to lay there for thirty minutes, then flip over for another thirty minutes. After that, though, I want to start raking the beach. I want to clean something up. I want to do something. To think I would lay on a beach every day for years and years, come on. That's fantasyland stuff.

What we're really talking about is living your life. Work is trading out making money for your life. You need to be enjoying your life, while in the process of living your life. We always praise someone for scoring a touchdown. We reward someone for closing a big deal. It's always about the end result.

What is missed, especially in the United States, is the process. We don't appreciate all the work it took to make that touchdown, all the sacrifices that had to be made to close that big deal. We don't value all the thought and work it took to build something. All we look at are the end results, and we need to start looking at the process, too.

You need to enjoy the process, the daily and hourly process of moving toward your goals. That's what excites me. I'm in love with the process. Even though it's still hard for me.

I recall a story about a couple that traveled to a beautiful island. They headed out on a two-hour journey to reach the main town. Along the way, they drove down the coast where they stopped to look at whales. They drove a little further and pulled over to see dolphins frolicking in the ocean. Still further down the coast, they paused and were amazed when they saw a bale of sea turtles sunbathing on the rocks. Once they left the coast, they traveled through a beautiful countryside where they lingered at a small waterfall, taking in the wonders of nature.

Finally, after hours of driving, they reached their destination. It was a tiny town with one store, very few houses, and almost no people. Upon seeing this, the wife sighed and lamented, "Well, this is disappointing." The thing that's really sad is that she missed the entire point. The destination wasn't the point. The journey itself was the point.

Are you enjoying the journey? Don't miss your life. If all you're focused on is getting to the next level or making a certain amount of money, I believe you're going to be sadly disappointed when you finally get there. You're going to work when you shouldn't be working. You're going to be focused on the end result when you should be enjoying your life and what it takes to get there. You're going to spend your whole life working and you're going to miss life.

All the time, I hear people say, "I can't wait until my kids can talk or walk," "I can't wait until they start school, graduate, or start college," "I can't wait until they're eighteen years old, twenty-one years old, or they're getting married." Time with your children goes by in the blink of an eye. You need to enjoy every day and every step along the way. You need to fall in love with the process along the way.

I've never met anybody that said they gave it everything they had for a year and just didn't make it. I have never talked to a single person that has said that. I have, however, met thousands of people that have said they're just going to dip their toe in it to see if it works out. I've heard countless people say they'll try it for three months or even six months. That is an insane way of thinking something will work out.

You may question, what if it doesn't work? Here's the thing: If you're in the right system, in the right kind of business, and you love what you're doing, you're going to make it. I can tell you; you're going to make it.

Even so, you can't go in with the wrong attitude. You can't go into it thinking you're going to quit if it doesn't work out by a certain time, if you don't make a certain amount of money, if you don't get the promotion, whatever it is. You also cannot walk in with the attitude of quitting after you reach a certain arbitrary goal. It's never going to end. You need to understand that life will keep going, and you have to enjoy the process. When God said, "Be still and know that I am God," He must have known how hard this is (Psalm 46:10).

If you haven't ever made God part of your equation in your life, I encourage you to make Him a priority to pursue. He makes all the difference.

Action: Stop now and rub your fingers together for twenty seconds. What does it feel like? Notice the texture, sound, feel, etc. This forces your brain to be in the present.

CHAPTER 19

Funny Stories

"If you think hiring a professional is expensive, wait till you hire an amateur."

-Red Adair

These are some of the funny things that could happen to you and some of them you should avoid.

One of my new agents, Susy, who was super aggressive and not afraid of much, got a call to show a property to some new clients. She called me on her way to the showing around 6:30 p.m.. I asked all my usual questions, "Do you know them?" "Where is the house?" and "Are you taking someone with you to the showing?" No, she didn't know them, the house was out in the county in an area we didn't know much about, and she was alone. I advised her to wait, but she assured me that it would be okay. I told her to give me the address as soon as she got there and to stay on the phone until she saw them and got a feeling of whether it was safe.

The first thing that happened was she pulled up to the property that had a gate with a chain wrapped around it. It was pretty much already dark outside. She had me on the phone and started unraveling the chain. Then she screamed and dropped her phone. A large Great Dane had jumped up on her back and put its paws on her shoulders! The clients weren't there yet. She finally saw them driving up and I lost the call. I tried over and over to call her back and called her husband to see if he knew what address she went to. In about thirty-five minutes, she called me back. She said it all went well and that she thought they were going to put in an offer.

2)   Todd received a call from an unknown caller wanting him to come over and see what his house might be worth. Todd got the address and went over to the house to find it reeking of hoarder status. The man had long, stringy hair, dirty clothes, and was dragging an oxygen bottle behind him. As the man showed Todd the house, Todd was not letting the guy get behind him or walking into any rooms in front of him. They finally worked their way to the back of the house where the kitchen is located. Todd noticed a large dog laying in the room and asked if the dog bites. The old guy said, "Nah, I had him stuffed 'cause I liked him so much."

3) I had a client that wanted to buy a house in a neighborhood that was very cookie cutter. Big production builders like to build the same house over and over because it saves them money. I showed my client about four houses in this neighborhood. She decided she wanted the one that backed up to an empty field. I wrote the offer and it was accepted. My client wanted the kitchen painted as part of the deal. I also noticed that the entry had a broken tile and I asked them if they would fix that also. About three weeks before closing, I went over to see if they had completed the work. First thing I noticed was that the tile had not been repaired. I called the seller and asked when they were going to do it. The lady told me that they didn't see a broken tile. I thought it was impossible for them not to have seen it. I also noticed that the kitchen was not painted. She told me they had already painted it red. Something was really off. I started looking at the contract I wrote. There were two houses on the same street across from each other. I had written the offer on the wrong house. Everything did work out fine. They liked the color so well in the other house, they left it and it sold also.

4) I used to flip houses with one of the guys that worked with me at Hobby Lobby Jeff. Jeff was in his mid thirties when I was buying houses and he would go do a majority of the work. I bought this house in Bridge Creek right off a busy street. The only story I had heard about the house was the owner weighed over 600 lbs. and could not leave the house. Jeff and his wife, Angie, had been married for about ten years at this time. They had grown up and dated in this area. Angie was cleaning out the house and came across an old camera that they found on the side of the highway when they were dating. She just left the camera in a drawer for ten years. She decided to develop the film. Well guess what, it was photos of the guy and inside of the house that we were about to sell. I'm not sure to this day what God was trying to let me in on.

CHAPTER 20

My Wife and My Life

*"You can make money or you can make excuses.
Which do you prefer?"*

-Tom Ferry

My book wouldn't be complete without expanding a little more about my wife. I would love to say that my wife was my childhood sweetheart and I've been married for forty years, but that's not the case. Unfortunately, divorce happens, which is how my first marriage ended. The second time around, I was lucky enough to find the love of my life, and it feels like I've always been married to her. You need to know that before I start my story, because it has an impact when I talk about my wife and my wife's faith.

My wife has never been involved in my business. That being said, she has made major impacts in my life that have to be recognized. Even though she would never take credit for it, she is the motivation behind my success. She drives me, and it's because of her we have what we have and our kids are what they are today.

I talked earlier in the book about my oldest son and his addiction, which caused him to need a heart transplant. An operation like that requires a lot of after-care. I live what I preach, and I was getting Kevo Properties up and running which required most of my attention. I loved my son, of course, and devoted as much spare time as possible but the credit goes to my wife for helping him to get back on his feet. Unfortunately, his addiction later claimed his life. Yet, if not for my wife, he probably wouldn't have made it out of the hospital that first round.

While all that was happening with my son, my wife was diagnosed with Stage 3 breast cancer. For the next three years, she fought this horrible disease. She had a double mastectomy, along with full radiation and chemotherapy. I can happily say she has been cancer-free for over five years now, which is incredible! She's healthy and more gorgeous than ever.

Here's what makes her so amazing. Even when she was at her sickest going through chemotherapy, most people didn't know what was going on. We still had four kids at home, and they didn't even realize how sick she was through most of it because she was so tough and didn't whine. When her hair began falling out, she shaved it off and wore wigs. She was absolutely unbelievable during the entire process.

Our life has become magical. We go on five or six trips a year, visiting places we never thought we would. That's not the best thing about being successful and making money, though. The best thing is you don't have to worry about house payments, car payments, or the electric bill. All that stuff just disappears. It's something you never have to think about again. And more importantly, the stress of worrying how to make the house payment or pay the bills is gone. You can't put a price on that.

Keep your faith at all times and realize that you will go through tough times. But once you go through something tough and make it to the other side, your character has been built. It gives you a strength and a faith that you never believed you could have. And that can never be taken from you.

What wears me down faster than anything is the mental aspect of the job. You can be physically fit, but if your faith isn't in line, it won't make a difference. If you're a believer, a follower of Christ, God pursues you. When you put Him first, "seek Him first," then all the "things" are added to you ... love, peace, joy, patience, goodness, faithfulness, kindness, gentleness, self-control (Galatians 5:22-23). That's called the fruit of the Spirit.

Finally ... The good news is that there isn't a "finish line" to cross over when you're in business for yourself. If you've learned anything about me from this book, you've learned that the journey is the best part of life. Yes, there are achievements and goals, but there is nothing to "finish." You've also learned that it's possible to enjoy your life in the middle of the toughest storms of your life. Not that it's easy, and not that every day is roses and sunshine. Every day is a gift though. You and I woke up today and we've been given this day. What will we do with it? As for me and my house, we will serve the Lord and we will make the most of all He's given us.

CHAPTER 21

Finally Home

"Practice saying this: I sell real estate and yes…
I am good at it!"

-Steve Burris

Home. There's no place like it. What truly makes a home? Is it the beautiful decor or the paint colors? Is it the location or size? Whether in a few hundred square feet or ten thousand, a "home" includes a batch of ingredients. Ask one hundred people what those ingredients are and you'll receive a hundred different lists. Recently a survey of a thousand people in the UK were asked to rank the top thirty things of what makes a house a home. Among the list was what we would expect: family, pets, comfy furniture, etc. There were also a few surprises such as general noise, clean sheets, a few arguments—yes, 18 percent of those surveyed added that to their top thirty.

When you stop to really look around you, what would be at the top of your list? Where would you rank your kids and clean sheets? As you move into making the decision to become a REALTOR®, these will all be considerations you'll help your clients with in their decision-making process. Real estate brings people home, and your job helps make that possible.

Along the way on your journey, I hope you'll pick up my book when you need a kick-in-the-pants or a high five. Essentially, they provide the same motivation, one just feels better than the other.

When you began reading, I mentioned my goal with Kevo Properties was to turn the real estate world on its head. We focus on our agents in order to provide the best training, and in turn, provide the best outcome for our agents. In addition, I want you to be the thirteen out of a hundred that represents those who will succeed in this industry, instead of the eighty-seven that fail. Match that with the concept that not only can you succeed, but you can thrive ... and your life will change. Your dreams can come true!

Action: Review the action steps at the end of each chapter. Do any that you might have missed.

Made in the USA
Middletown, DE
08 October 2023